Eliot Attridge, Adam Bayley, Andrew McAdam, Dorothy V̄ ⋯ ⋯ and Steve Wiseman

REVISION PLUS

OCR Twenty First Century
GCSE Science A
Revision and Classroom Companion

Ideas about Science

Introduction to Ideas about Science

The OCR Twenty First Century Science specification aims to ensure that you develop an understanding of science itself – of how scientific knowledge is obtained, the kinds of evidence and reasoning behind it, its strengths and limitations, and how far we can rely on it.

These issues are explored through Ideas about Science, which are built into the specification content and summarised over the following pages.

The tables below give an overview of the Ideas about Science that can be assessed in each unit and provide examples of content which support them in this guide.

Unit A161 (Modules B1, B2 and B3)

Ideas about Science	Example of Supporting Content
Cause–effect explanations	Variation (page 3)
Developing scientific explanations	Evolution (page 28)
The scientific community	Evolution (page 28)
Risk	Risks (page 13)
Making decisions about science and technology	Reliability (page 9)

Unit A171 (Modules C1, C2 and C3)

Ideas about Science	Example of Supporting Content
Data: their importance and limitations	Data about Pollution (pages 33–34)
Cause–effect explanations	Identifying Health Hazards (page 37)
Developing scientific explanations	The Origins of Mineral Wealth in Britain (page 46)
The scientific community	Identifying Health Hazards (page 37)
Risk	Food and the Government (page 51); Safe and Sustainable Chemicals (page 54)
Making decisions about science and technology	Evaluating Nanomaterials (page 45); Life Cycle Assessment (LCA) (page 55)

Unit A181 (Modules P1, P2 and P3)

Ideas about Science	Example of Supporting Content
Cause–effect explanations	Tectonic Plates (page 63)
Developing scientific explanations	Global Warming (page 73)
The scientific community	Radiation Protection (page 71)
Risk	Radiation Protection (page 71)
Making decisions about science and technology	Generating Electricity (page 77)

① Data: Their Importance and Limitations

Science is built on data. Scientists carry out experiments to collect and interpret data, seeing whether the data agree with their explanations. If the data do agree, then it means the current explanation is more likely to be correct. If not, then the explanation has to be changed.

Experiments aim to find out what the 'true' value of a quantity is. Quantities are affected by errors made when carrying out the experiment and random variation. This means that the measured value may be different to the true value. Scientists try to control all the factors that could cause this uncertainty.

Scientists always take repeat readings to try to make sure that they have accurately estimated the true value of a quantity. The mean is calculated and is the best estimate of what the true value of a quantity is. The more times an experiment is repeated, the greater the chance that a result near to the true value will fall within the mean.

The range, or spread, of data gives an indication of where the true value must lie. Sometimes a measurement will not be in the zone where the majority of readings fall. It may look like the result (called an 'outlier') is wrong – however, it does not automatically mean that it is. The outlier has to be checked by repeating the measurement of that quantity. If the result cannot be checked, then it should still be used.

Here is an example of an outlier in a set of data:

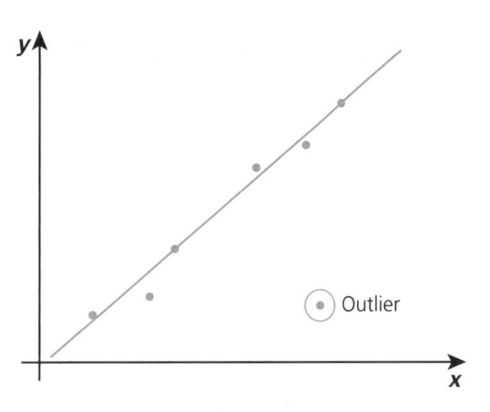

HT The spread of the data around the mean (the range) gives an idea of whether it really is different to the mean from another measurement. If the ranges for each mean do not overlap, then it is more likely that the two means are different. However, sometimes the ranges do overlap and there may be no significant difference between them.

The ranges also give an indication of reliability – a wide range makes it more difficult to say with certainty that the true value of a quantity has been measured. A small range suggests that the mean is closer to the true value.

If an outlier is discovered, you need to be able to defend your decision as to whether you keep it or discard it.

② Cause–effect Explanations

Science is based on the idea that a factor has an effect on an outcome. Scientists make predictions as to how the input variable will change the outcome variable. To make sure that only the input variable can affect the outcome, scientists try to control all the other variables that could potentially alter it. This is called 'fair testing'.

You need to be able to explain why it is necessary to control all the factors that might affect the outcome. This means suggesting how they could influence the outcome of the experiment.

A correlation is where there is an apparent link between a factor and an outcome. It may be that as the factor increases, the outcome increases as well. On the other hand, it may be that when the factor increases, the outcome decreases.

For example, there is a correlation between temperature and the rate of rusting – the higher the temperature, the faster the rate of rusting.

Just because there is a correlation does not necessarily mean that the factor causes the outcome. Further experiments are needed to establish this. It could be that another factor causes the outcome or that both the original factor and outcome are caused by something else.

The following graph suggests a correlation between going to the opera regularly and living longer. It is far more likely that if you have the money to go to the opera, you can afford a better diet and health care. Going to the opera is not the true cause of the correlation.

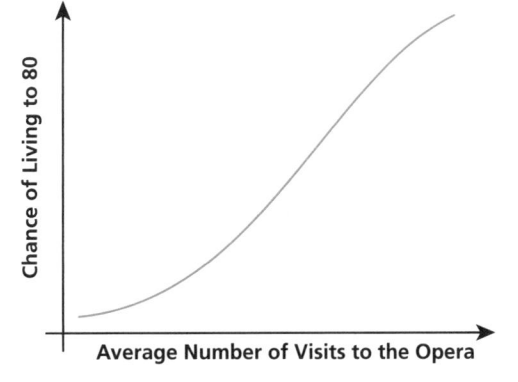

Sometimes the factor may alter the chance of an outcome occurring but does not guarantee it will lead to it. The statement 'the more time spent on a sun bed the greater the chance of developing skin cancer' is an example of this type of correlation, as some people will not develop skin cancer even if they do spend a lot of time on a sun bed.

To investigate claims that a factor increases the chance of an outcome, scientists have to study groups of people who either share as many factors as possible or are chosen randomly to try to ensure that all factors will present in people in the test group. The larger the experimental group, the more confident scientists can be about the conclusions made.

Ideas about Science

❸ Developing Scientific Explanations

Scientists devise hypotheses (predictions of what will happen in an experiment), along with an explanation (the scientific mechanism behind the hypotheses) and theories (that can be tested).

Explanations involve thinking creatively to work out why data have a particular pattern. Good scientific explanations account for most or all of the data already known. Sometimes they may explain a range of phenomena that were not previously thought to be linked. Explanations should enable predictions to be made about new situations or examples.

When deciding on which is the better of two explanations, you should be able to give reasons why.

Explanations are tested by comparing predictions based on them with data from observations or experiments. If there is an agreement between the experimental findings, then it increases the chance of the explanation being right. However, it does not prove it is correct. Likewise, if the prediction and observation indicate that one or the other is wrong, it decreases the confidence in the explanation on which the prediction is based.

❹ The Scientific Community

Once a scientist has carried out enough experiments to back up his/her claims, they have to be reported. This enables the scientific community to carefully check the claims, something which is required before they are accepted as scientific knowledge.

Scientists attend conferences where they share their findings and sound out new ideas and explanations. This can lead to scientists revisiting their work or developing links with other laboratories to improve it.

The next step is writing a formal scientific paper and submitting it to a journal in the relevant field. The paper is allocated to peer reviewers (experts in their field), who carefully check and evaluate the paper. If the peer reviewers accept the paper, then it is published. Scientists then read the paper and check the work themselves.

New scientific claims that have not been evaluated by the whole scientific community have less credibility than well-established claims. It takes time for other scientists to gather enough evidence that a theory is sound. If the results cannot be repeated or replicated by themselves or others, then scientists will be sceptical about the new claims.

If the explanations cannot be arrived at from the available data, then it is fair and reasonable for different scientists to come up with alternative explanations. These will be based on the background and experience of the scientists. It is through further experimentation that the best explanation will be chosen.

This means that the current explanation has the greatest support. New data are not enough to topple it. Only when the new data are sufficiently repeated and checked will the original explanation be changed.

❺ Risk

Everything we do (or not do) carries risk. Nothing is completely risk-free. New technologies and processes based on scientific advances often introduce new risks.

Risk is sometimes calculated by measuring the chance of something occurring in a large sample over a given period of time (calculated risk). This enables people to take informed decisions about whether the risk is worth taking. In order to decide, you have to balance the benefit (to individuals or groups) with the consequences of what could happen.

For example, deciding whether or not to add chlorine to drinking water involves weighing up the benefit (of reducing the spread of cholera) against the risk of a toxic chlorine leak at the purification plant.

Risk which is associated with something that someone has chosen to do is easier to accept than risk which has been imposed on them.

> **HT** Perception of risk changes depending on our personal experience (perceived risk). Familiar risks (e.g. using bleach without wearing gloves) tend to be under-estimated, whilst unfamiliar risks (e.g. making chlorine in the laboratory) and invisible or long-term risks (e.g. cleaning up mercury from a broken thermometer) tend to be over-estimated.
>
> For example, many people under-estimate the risk that adding limescale remover and bleach to a toilet at the same time might produce toxic chlorine gas.

Governments and public bodies try to assess risk and create policy on what is and what is not acceptable. This can be controversial, especially when the people who benefit most are not the ones at risk.

6 Making Decisions about Science and Technology

Science has helped to create new technologies that have improved the world, benefiting millions of people. However, there can be unintended consequences of new technologies, even many decades after they were first introduced. These could be related to the impact on the environment or to the quality of life.

When introducing new technologies, the potential benefits must be weighed up against the risks.

Sometimes unintended consequences affecting the environment can be identified. By applying the scientific method (making hypotheses, explanations and carrying out experiments), scientists can devise new ways of putting right the impact. Devising life cycle assessments helps scientists to try to minimise unintended consequences and ensure sustainability.

Some areas of science could have a high potential risk to individuals or groups if they go wrong or if they are abused. In these areas the Government ensures that regulations are in place.

The scientific approach covers anything where data can be collected and used to test a hypothesis. It cannot be used when evidence cannot be collected (e.g. it cannot test beliefs or values).

Just because something can be done does not mean that it should be done. Some areas of scientific research or the technologies resulting from them have ethical issues associated with them. This means that not all people will necessarily agree with it.

Ethical decisions have to be made, taking into account the views of everyone involved, whilst balancing the benefits and risks.

It is impossible to please everybody, so decisions are often made on the basis of which outcome will benefit most people. Within a culture there will also be some actions that are always right or wrong, no matter what the circumstances are.

Contents

Module B1 (You and Your Genes)

Many of an individual's characteristics are inherited from their two biological parents. This module looks at:

- genes and their effect on development
- how understanding genetic information can be used to prevent disease
- how genetic information can and should be used.

Genetic Information

All organisms develop following a set of instructions that are coded inside the cell in the nucleus. The instructions control how the organism develops and functions. The basic unit for the instructions is called the **gene**. Genes occur in very long **DNA** (deoxyribonucleic acid) molecules called **chromosomes**.

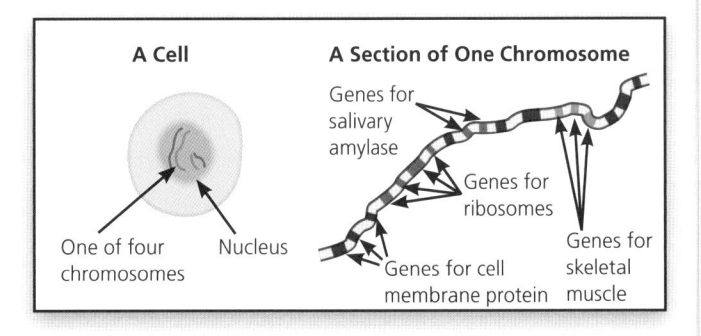

A Cell

One of four chromosomes   Nucleus

A Section of One Chromosome

Genes for salivary amylase

Genes for ribosomes

Genes for cell membrane protein

Genes for skeletal muscle

Chromosomes are made of DNA molecules. Each DNA molecule consists of two strands, which form a **double helix**.

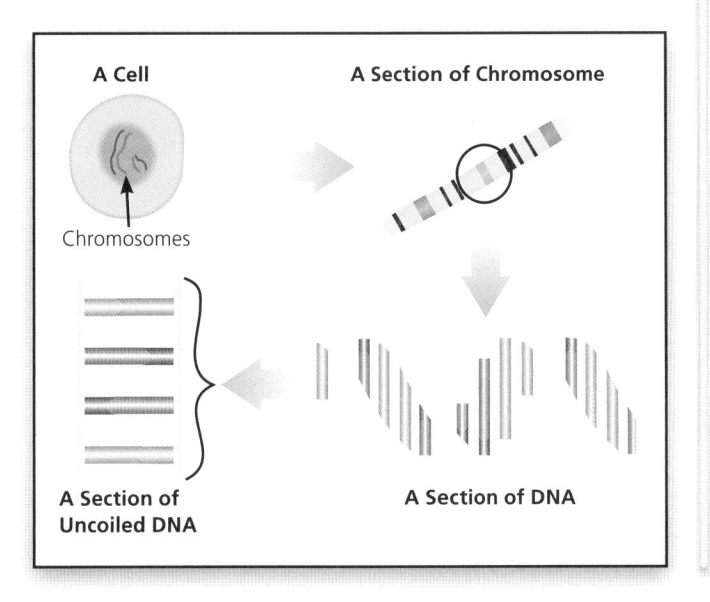

A Cell

Chromosomes

A Section of Chromosome

A Section of Uncoiled DNA

A Section of DNA

Genes are sections of DNA that describe how to make proteins. These may be structural (e.g. for collagen in skin) or functional (e.g. for enzymes such as amylase, which breaks down starch). Some characteristics are coded for by a number of genes that work together, e.g. eye colour.

Eye Colour

Originally it was believed that eye colour was due to a single gene. It is now known that there are a number of genes coding for the different pigments in the iris, mainly on chromosome 15 in humans. This means that there is an enormous variation in eye colour.

Variation

The differences between individuals of the same species are described as **variations**.

Variation may be due to:
- **genes** – the different characteristics that an individual inherits, e.g. whether you have dimples or not
- **environmental factors** – how the environment changes an individual, e.g. cutting the skin may cause a scar.

Dimple   Scar

Variation is usually due to a combination of genes and the environment, e.g. your weight. Biologists carry out a lot of research to try to determine whether a characteristic is genetic or environmental. Even if a gene is discovered, it does not mean that it is the only factor in that characteristic.

Genotype is the term describing the genetic makeup of an organism (the combination of alleles). **Phenotype** describes the observable characteristics the organism has.

Alleles

All body cells contain pairs of chromosomes. The genes in each chromosome are in the same place on each one, which means that body cells usually have two copies of each gene. These copies of each gene can be different versions, called **alleles**.

Alleles are described as being either **dominant** or **recessive**. A dominant allele is one that controls the development of a characteristic even if it is present on only one chromosome in a pair. A recessive allele controls the development of a characteristic only if the dominant allele is not present, i.e. both chromosomes have the recessive allele present.

The allele of a gene is usually represented by a letter. If the allele is dominant, it is denoted by a capital letter. If the allele is recessive, it is denoted by a lower-case letter. As each body cell has two alleles for each gene, they can be the same or different.

For example, the ability to roll your tongue is dominant so it can be represented by T. If your alleles were TT or Tt, then you would be able to roll your tongue. If your alleles were tt, you would not be able to roll your tongue.

If you carried one of each allele then you would not express the recessive characteristic. You would be a carrier for that allele but would have the dominant allele expressed.

When the two alleles are the same we say that they are **homozygous**. When they are different they are **heterozygous**. For example, TT = homozygous dominant; tt = homozygous recessive; Tt = heterozygous.

Sex Cells

The **sex cells**, eggs produced by the **ovaries** in females and sperm produced by the **testes** in males, only carry one copy of each chromosome. This is the basis of sexual reproduction.

Humans have 23 pairs of chromosomes in their body cells (46 in total). The sex cells have half the amount, i.e. 23 single chromosomes.

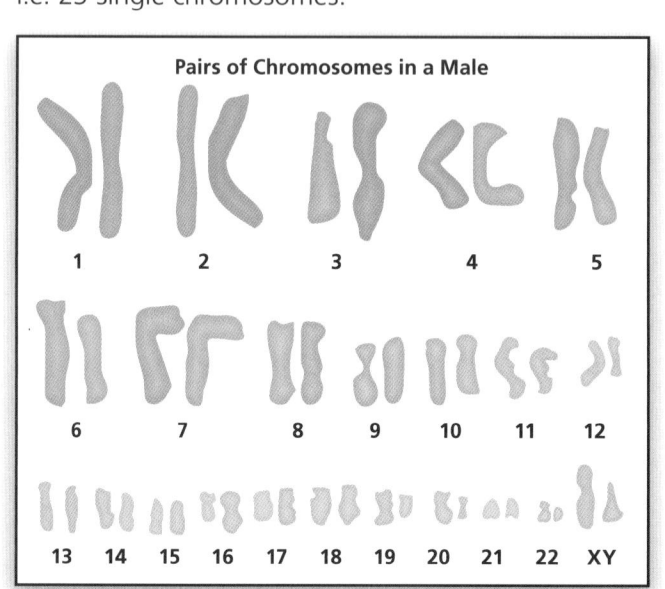

Pairs of Chromosomes in a Male

1 2 3 4 5
6 7 8 9 10 11 12
13 14 15 16 17 18 19 20 21 22 XY

This means that when fertilisation takes place (i.e. the nuclei of the sperm and the egg fuse), the total number of chromosomes doubles as they pair up again.

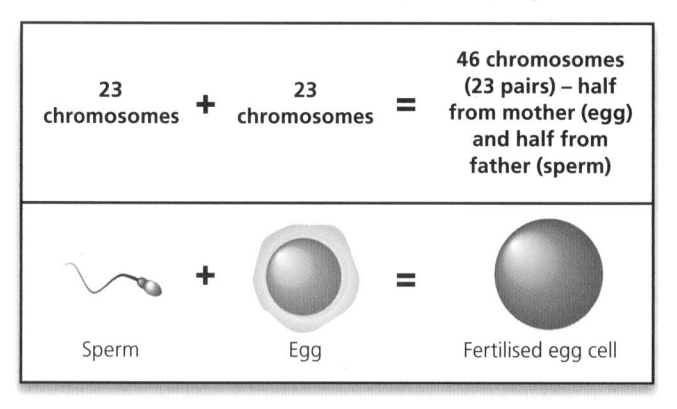

| 23 chromosomes | + | 23 chromosomes | = | 46 chromosomes (23 pairs) – half from mother (egg) and half from father (sperm) |

Sperm + Egg = Fertilised egg cell

As the pairing up of the chromosomes is random, the new offspring will differ from its parents. This leads to variation, a major advantage of sexual reproduction. The child will share similarities with its parents depending on which characteristics have come from the father, which have come from the mother and which ones are dominant and recessive. The child will also differ from any brothers and sisters.

Genetic Diagrams

It is easiest to follow what is happening with the inheritance of gene characteristics by drawing genetic diagrams.

Family trees can be used to trace the inheritance of a characteristic and to work out who must have been carrying a faulty allele.

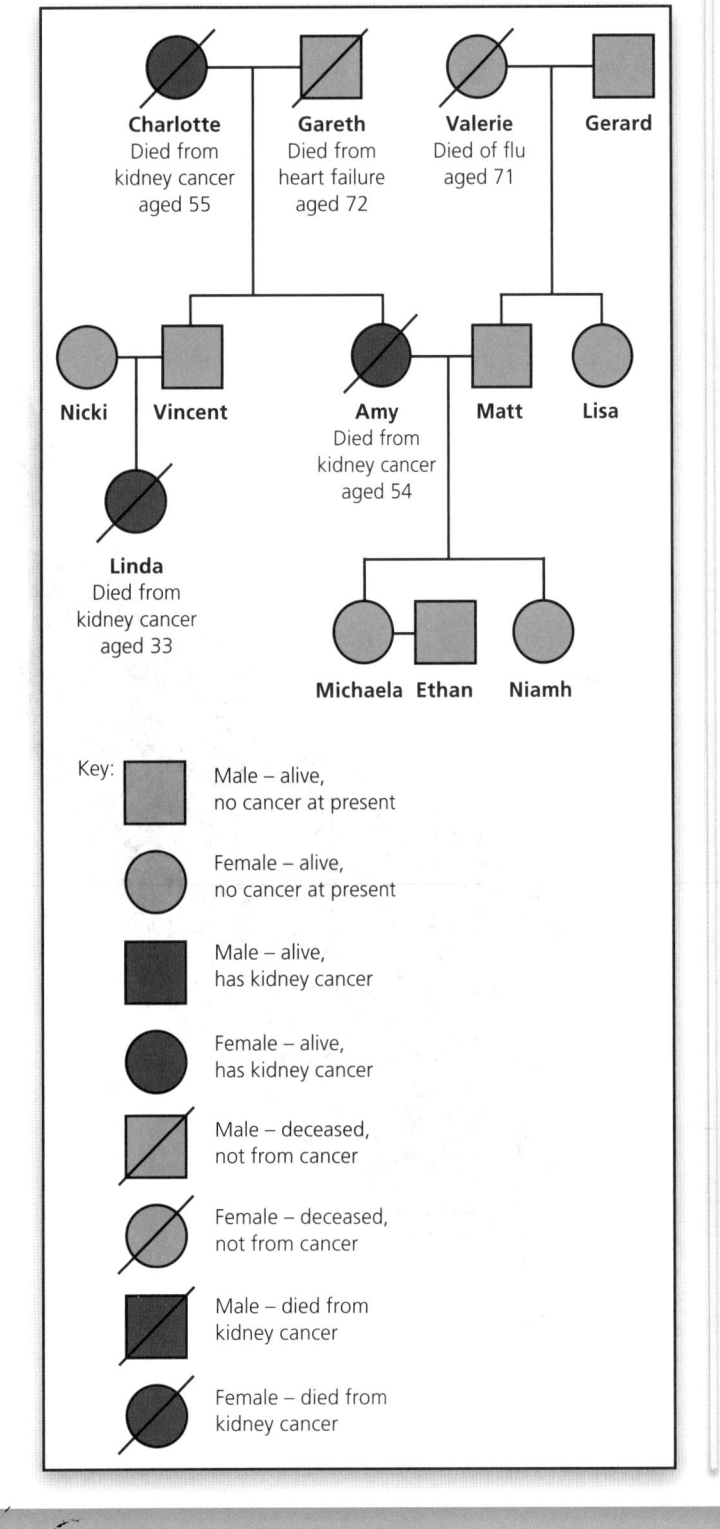

Key:

☐ (grey square) Male – alive, no cancer at present

◯ (grey circle) Female – alive, no cancer at present

■ (dark square) Male – alive, has kidney cancer

● (dark circle) Female – alive, has kidney cancer

▨ (grey square, slash) Male – deceased, not from cancer

◯̸ (grey circle, slash) Female – deceased, not from cancer

■̸ (dark square, slash) Male – died from kidney cancer

●̸ (dark circle, slash) Female – died from kidney cancer

As Amy had kidney cancer, it is possible she carried both recessive alleles. Michaela would be worried as she would suspect that she may have inherited one of the alleles from Amy. As the cancer must be due to a homozygous recessive allele, she would be correct. If Matt was also a carrier, then Michaela would have the chance that she has both alleles causing the cancer.

When looking at the possibilities of inheriting an allele, we can use a **Punnett square diagram**. This shows all the possible pairings of alleles from sperm and egg at fertilisation.

With a Punnett square, the possible versions of sperm and egg are placed at the sides and the possible offspring that could result are plotted.

For example, if a male with a dominant **A** allele and recessive **a** allele was to mate with a female with the same alleles, the following diagram could be drawn:

		♂	
		A	**a**
♀	**A**	AA	Aa
	a	Aa	aa

This means that three of the four possible offspring would show the dominant characteristic while only one of the four possible offspring would be recessive for both alleles.

> **HT** The diagram shows that the possible genotypes would be one homozygous dominant offspring, two heterozygous offspring and one homozygous recessive offspring.
>
> The genotypes would be in the ratio 1 : 2 : 1. The ratio of the phenotypes would be 3 : 1 (three dominant to one recessive).

Sex Chromosomes

One of the 23 pairs of chromosomes in a human cell is the sex chromosome. In females the sex chromosomes are the same – they are both X chromosomes. In males they are different – there is an X chromosome and a Y chromosome. The Y chromosome is much shorter than the X chromosome.

We can draw a Punnett square to represent how sex is determined. This time, rather than an allele, we are writing the whole chromosome that will be carried by the sperm or egg (X or Y).

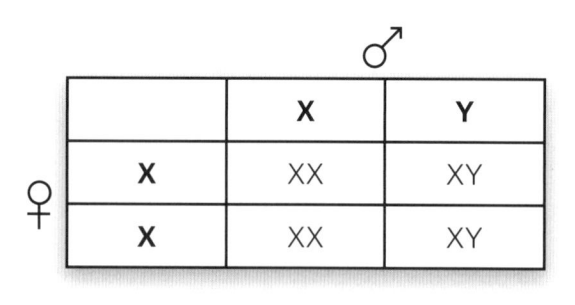

		♂	
		X	**Y**
♀	**X**	XX	XY
	X	XX	XY

Therefore, 50% of the offspring will be female and 50% male. As the process of fertilisation is completely random, some families will only have girls whilst others will only have boys.

Rare Disorders

Most characteristics are governed by a range of genes, so the presence of one 'faulty' allele may not affect the overall outcome.

Usually, disorders are caused by a recessive gene, but occasionally the faulty gene is dominant, meaning that only one allele needs to be present for the disorder to be expressed.

For example, **Huntington's disease** is caused by the presence of a single dominant faulty allele. This means that if a parent carries the dominant allele, then the child has a 50% chance of carrying it too.

Cystic fibrosis, on the other hand, is caused by the presence of a faulty recessive allele. Both recessive alleles are needed for the disease to develop.

Sex Determination

The sex of an embryo is determined by a gene on the Y chromosome called the SRY (sex-determining region Y) gene.

If the gene is not present, i.e. if there are two X chromosomes present, the embryo will develop into a female and ovaries will grow. If the gene is present, i.e. if both an X and a Y chromosome are present, then testes will begin to develop.

Six weeks after fertilisation, the undifferentiated gonads start producing a hormone called **androgen**. Specialised receptors in the developing embryo detect the androgen. This stimulates the male reproductive organs grow.

Sometimes the Y chromosome is present, but the androgen is *not* detected. When this happens, the embryo develops all the female sex organs except the uterus. The baby is born with a female body but will be infertile.

...dr...	...ndroge.. + detected
...ale	Genetically male
Appear... male	Appears female; no uterus

Huntington's Disease

Huntington's disease is a genetic disorder that affects the central nervous system. It is caused by a faulty dominant allele on chromosome 4.

The allele that causes the disease results in damage to nerve cells in certain areas of the brain. This leads to gradual physical, mental and emotional changes that are expressed as symptoms.

The symptoms of the disease normally develop in adulthood, which means sufferers may have already had children and passed on the gene. Symptoms include late onset, a tremor, clumsiness, memory loss, an inability to concentrate and mood changes.

Everyone who inherits the Huntington's allele will develop the disease. This is due to the allele being dominant. Only one parent needs to pass on the allele for a child to develop the disorder.

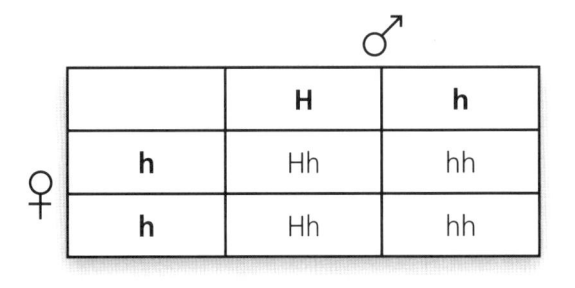

	♂ H	h
h	Hh	hh
h	Hh	hh

50% have Huntington's disease, 50% do not.

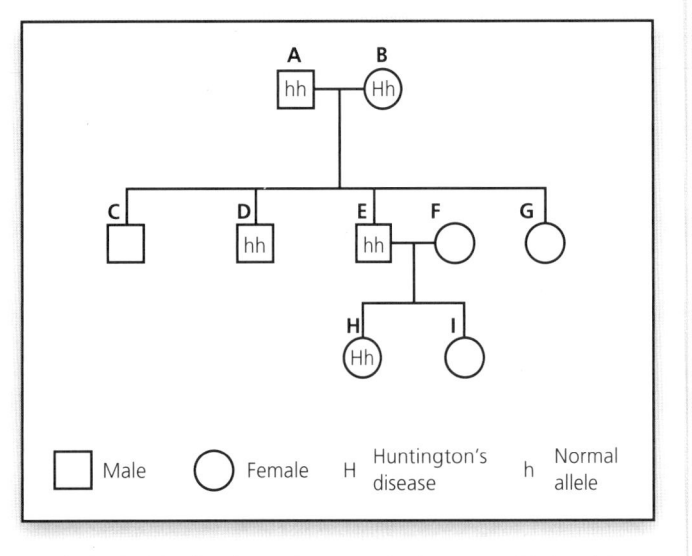

| Male | Female | H Huntington's disease | h Normal allele |

With individual I there is a 50% chance of inheriting the H allele if the mother (F) was Hh and 100% if she was HH.

Cystic Fibrosis

Cystic fibrosis is the UK's most common life-threatening genetic disease. It affects the cell membranes, causing a **thick mucus** to be produced in the lungs, gut and pancreas.

Other symptoms of cystic fibrosis are difficulty in breathing, an increased number of chest infections and difficulty in digesting food.

Although there is no cure at present, scientists have identified the faulty recessive allele that causes cystic fibrosis and are looking at ways to repair or replace it.

Unlike Huntington's disease, the cystic fibrosis allele is recessive. Therefore, if an individual is a carrier (has only one recessive allele) they will not have the characteristics of the disease. They can, however, pass on the allele to their children.

	♂ F	f
F	FF	Ff
F	FF	Ff

50% are carriers of the cystic fibrosis allele.

	♂ F	f
F	FF healthy	Ff carrier
f	Ff carrier	ff CF

25% are healthy, 50% are carriers and 25% will have cystic fibrosis.

Genetic Testing

It is now possible to test adults, children and embryos for a faulty allele if there is a family history of a genetic disorder. If the test turns out positive, the individual will have to decide whether or not to have children and risk passing on the disorder. This is called **predictive testing for genetic diseases**.

Genetic testing can also be carried out to determine whether an adult or child can be prescribed a particular drug without suffering from serious side effects.

For example, certain people are highly susceptible to getting liver damage while taking COX-2 (an enzyme in the body) inhibitor drugs. A genetic test would ensure that *only* those patients who do *not* have the susceptibility gene are prescribed the drug.

Embryos can be tested for embryo selection. The healthy embryos that do not have the faulty allele are then implanted. This process involves harvesting egg cells from the mother and then fertilising them with the father's sperm. Only the healthy embryos are implanted into the mother's uterus, where the pregnancy progresses as normal. This process is called ***in vitro* fertilisation** (IVF).

> **HT** The procedure for embryo selection is called **pre-implantation genetic diagnosis** (PGD). After fertilisation, the embryos are allowed to divide into eight cells before a single cell is removed from each one for testing. The selected cell is then tested to see if it carries the alleles for a specific genetic disease, i.e. the allele for the disease that one of the parents carries.
>
> The PGD test is not without risk – the result may be inaccurate and lead to a healthy embryo not being implanted. It may also decrease the chance of the embryo surviving once it has been implanted.

Risks of Genetic Testing

Testing is not without risk. When a fetus is tested, there is a risk that the test itself could cause the death of the fetus. There are two ways to carry out a test on a developing fetus:

1 Amniocentesis Testing

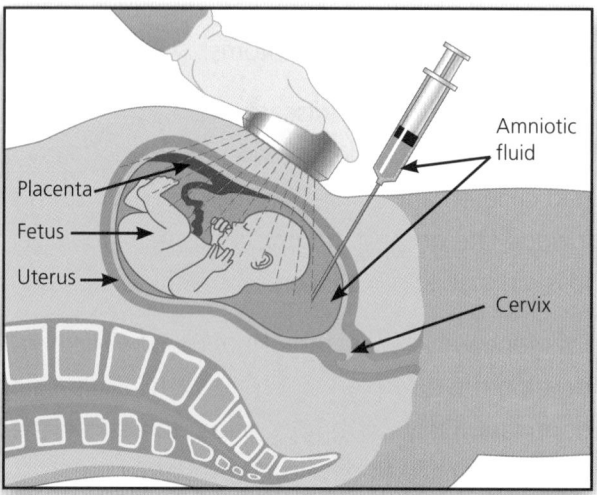

The amniocentesis test can be carried out at 14–16 weeks of pregnancy. A needle is inserted into the uterus, taking care to avoid the fetus itself, and a small sample of amniotic fluid, which carries cells from the fetus, is extracted.

If the test is positive for a given disease, then the pregnancy (now at 16–18 weeks) could be terminated. There is approximately a 0.5% (1 in 200) chance of the test itself causing a miscarriage. There is also a very small chance of infection.

2 Chorionic Villus Testing

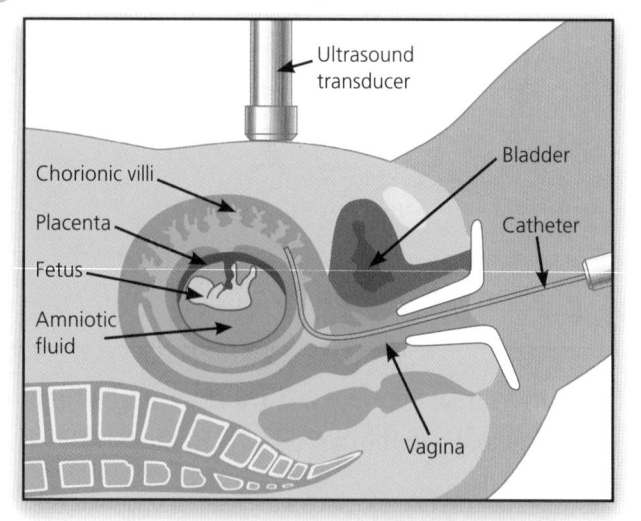

Chorionic villus sampling can take place earlier in pregnancy, at 8–10 weeks. A special catheter is inserted through the vagina and cervix until it reaches the placenta. Part of the placenta has finger-like protrusions called chorionic villi. Samples are removed for testing.

If the test is positive for the faulty allele then the pregnancy can be terminated much earlier (10–12 weeks). However, the chance of a miscarriage is much higher at approximately 2% (1 in 50).

Reliability

Because no test is 100% reliable, genetic testing can have a number of possible outcomes:

Outcome	Test Result	Reality
True positive	Subject has the disorder	Subject has the disorder
True negative	Subject does not have the disorder	Subject does not have the disorder
False positive	Subject has the disorder	Subject **does not** have the disorder
False negative	Subject does not have the disorder	Subject **has** the disorder

If the subject was a fetus, then the consequences of a false positive result could mean that the pregnancy was terminated, leading to the death of the fetus. On the other hand, a false negative result could lead to the birth of a baby with a severe genetic disease.

If the subject was a parent deciding whether or not to have children, the consequence of a false positive result could mean that the parent decides not to have children.

With all genetic tests, decisions also have to be taken as to whether other members of the family should be told of the test and the result. Although an individual might be willing to take a genetic test, other family members may not want to know.

For example, if a parent had a positive test for Huntington's disease, then there is at least a 50% chance that a child will also carry the allele. Should the child be told? Huntington's disease occurs late in life and is incurable. Is it fair to make someone worry about the condition decades before they are likely to get it?

These are **ethical considerations** and need to be considered carefully before decisions are taken.

There is always a difference between what *can* be done (i.e. what is technically possible) and what *should* be done (i.e. what is morally acceptable).

For example, governments may have the ability to impose genetic tests on individuals by implementing genetic screening programmes, but should they be allowed to do so?

There is the potential for genetic testing to be used to produce detailed genetic profiles. These could contain information on everything from an individual's ethnicity to whether they are susceptible to certain conditions (e.g. obesity) or diseases (e.g. cancer).

The question is: how will the information be used? Employers could potentially refuse to employ someone who possessed certain alleles and insurers may not cover a person who had genes that made them more likely to suffer a heart attack. Would this be fair?

Asexual Reproduction

When a cell grows and divides into two, it is a form of reproduction. As it does not involve sex, it is called **asexual reproduction**.

All bacteria reproduce asexually, as do many plants and some animals. As they are formed by the 'mother' cell dividing to form two 'daughter' cells, the genes in each cell are exactly the same. When an organism has exactly the same genetic information as another individual, it is called a **clone**.

The only differences between clones are due to the environment. For example, if a cloned plant received more water and sunlight than another, it would grow better.

Plants such as strawberries produce shoots called **runners**. These eventually break off and become new strawberry plants, clones of the original.

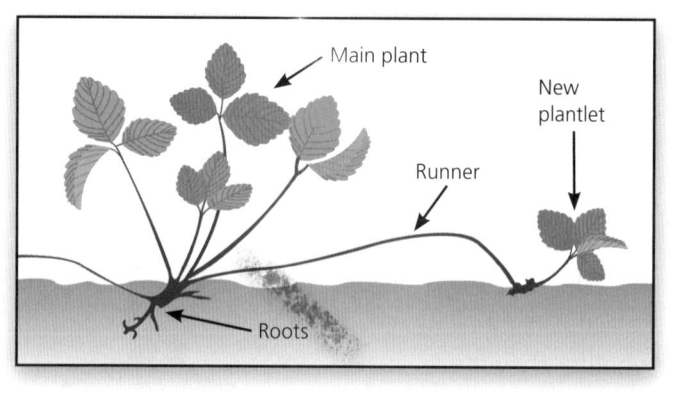

Other plants grow **bulbs**. When bulbs are planted they grow into genetically identical plants. Again the environment will alter them. No two organisms can occupy the same space in the universe so the environment will always be different for individuals, even if they are clones.

Clones of animals occur naturally when, during the earliest stages after fertilisation, the developing embryo splits into two. This leads to the creation of **identical twins**.

Identical triplets are also possible, although they are extremely rare. They occur when the fertilised egg splits into two and one of the new cells splits into two again.

It is now possible to make clones artificially by taking the nucleus from an adult body cell and transferring it into an empty, unfertilised egg cell. The process has been successful in a wide range of organisms, the most famous of which was a sheep named Dolly.

Stem Cells

Cloning depends on cells that have the potential to become any cell type in the body. These are called **stem cells**.

Adult stem cells are unspecialised cells that can develop into many, but not all, types of cell.

Embryonic stem cells are unspecialised cells that can develop into *any* type of cell, including more embryonic stem cells.

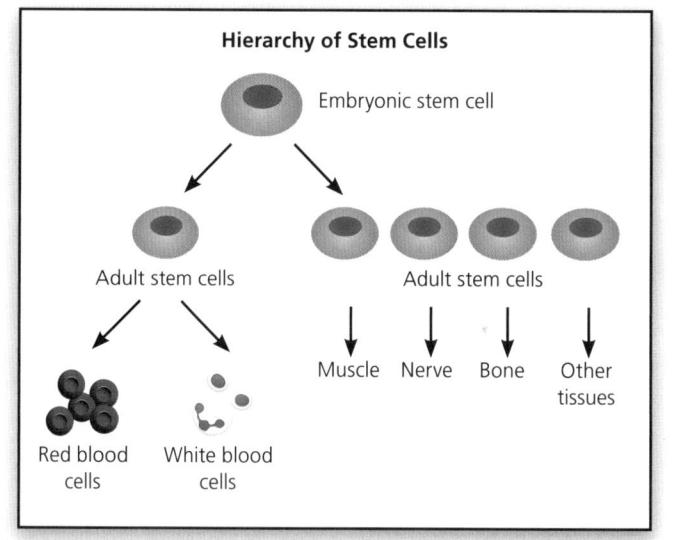

Both types of stem cell can be used to treat some illnesses or injuries. For example, skin can be grown as a treatment for serious burns and sight can now be restored to people who are blind due to damage of their corneas.

After the zygote has divided four times to reach the 16 cell stage, the majority of cells in the embryo start to become specialised. This means that certain genes are switched on and off. This leads to the production of proteins that are specific to the specialised cell type. Specialised cells can only divide to produce the same type of specialised cell.

Module B2 (Keeping Healthy)

To stay healthy it is important to maintain a healthy lifestyle and use medication when appropriate. This module looks at:

- how our bodies resist infection
- what vaccines are and how they work
- what antimicrobials are and why they can become less effective
- how new drugs are developed and tested
- what factors increase the risk of heart disease.

Microorganisms

Microorganisms are organisms that are too small to see with the naked eye. They include **bacteria**, **viruses** and **fungi**.

They can be beneficial to us (e.g. the bacteria that live in our intestines can produce certain vitamins) or they can cause us harm (e.g. bacteria that cause food poisoning).

Symptoms of Infectious Disease

Once inside the body, harmful microorganisms start to reproduce. As they grow in number they start to damage cells, often by bursting them (**lysis**). Sometimes they also produce toxins (poisons). When the damage to cells or the amount of toxin reaches a certain level then the symptoms of the disease will appear.

The human body provides ideal conditions for microorganisms to grow. In the body, there is water, oxygen (although not all microorganisms require this), food and heat, as well as different pH levels.

When the conditions are suitable, microorganisms can use these resources to reproduce very quickly. Some bacteria can take as little as 15 minutes to divide, meaning that they can increase rapidly in number. However, other bacteria can take days to divide.

This form of growth is known as **exponential growth**. It follows the formula:

$$x(t) = a \times b^{t/\tau}$$

where
x = the quantity of bacteria at a given time
a = amount of bacteria at start
b = growth factor
t = time
τ = time taken to double

For example, if a bacterium doubled every 20 minutes, how many would there be after an hour?

$a = 1$, $b = 2$, $t = 60$min and $\tau = 20$min

$$x(t) = a \times b^{t/\tau}$$
$$x(60\text{min}) = 1 \times 2^{60\text{min}/20\text{min}}$$
$$= 8$$

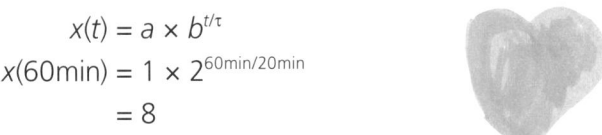

In four hours there would be 4096 bacteria; in 12 hours there would be 68 719 476 736 bacteria; and in 24 hours there would be 4.7×10^{21} bacteria.

In practice, these numbers would never be reached. The resources inside the body become less readily available as the number of bacteria increases.

A growth curve shows the realistic stages of bacterial growth:

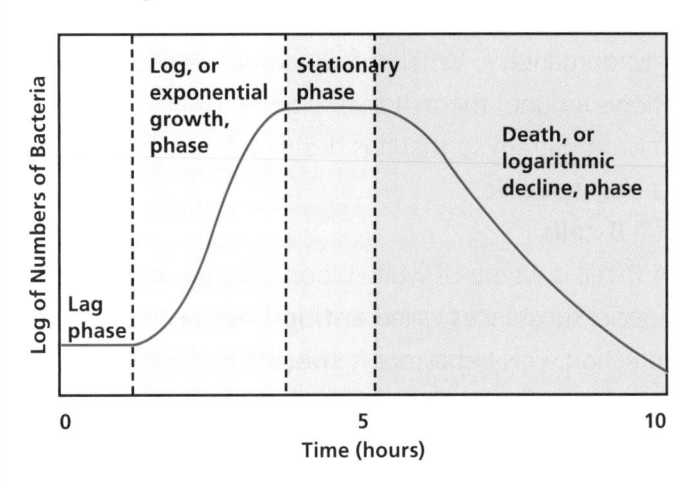

Using a soap that claimed to kill 99.9% of bacteria would reduce the original number by 1000 fold. So, if you had 8192 bacteria on your hands, washing would leave you with eight bacteria. However, they could still reproduce within a few hours to a great number.

The Immune System

The body has immune systems that defend it against invading microorganisms. These immune systems are layered, which means that as each defence is compromised there is a new layer for the microorganisms to try to break through.

Physical Barriers

In order to enter the body, microorganisms first have to breach the physical barriers. The skin is the first physical barrier – it has to be cut to allow entry. Sweat is another barrier – it has antimicrobial properties.

Other areas where microorganisms can enter include the eye (protected by chemicals in tears) and the stomach (where one of the functions of stomach acid is to sterilise the food, killing microorganisms).

The Immune Response

If microorganisms do breach the physical barriers then the immune system (the body's internal defence system) is activated. White blood cells play a major role in this response. There are a large number of white blood cell types, two of which are:

1 Neutrophils
A neutrophil is a type of white blood cell that moves around the body in the bloodstream looking for microorganisms. When it finds some, it engulfs (flows around) them. It then digests the microorganism so that it is destroyed. This behaviour is **non-specific**.

2 B-cells
A B-cell is a type of white blood cell that makes special substances called **antibodies** to combat infection. This behaviour is **specific** and leads to B-cells targeting the same organism if it invades again. They are, in effect, **memory cells**. B-cells travel mainly in the **lymphatic system**.

Antibodies and Antigens

Each microorganism has its own unique markers made out of protein on its surface. These markers are called **antigens**. The antibodies produced by

B-cells are specific to a particular antigen. For example, only TB antibodies will work with TB antigens; they will not work with the antigens from cholera.

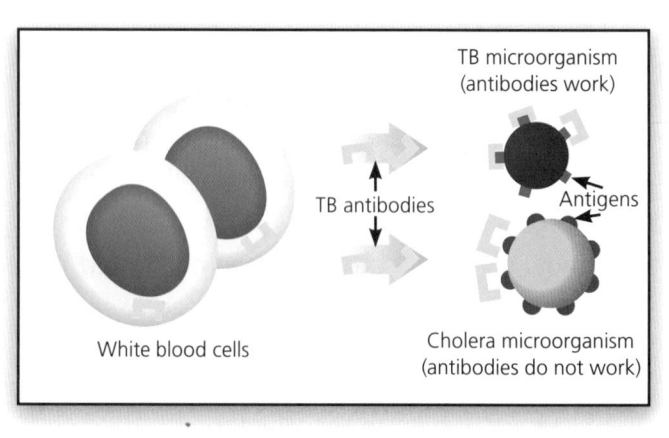

TB microorganism (antibodies work)

TB antibodies

Antigens

White blood cells

Cholera microorganism (antibodies do not work)

Once the invading microorganisms have been identified by antibodies, other white blood cells can consume them, ridding the body of the disease.

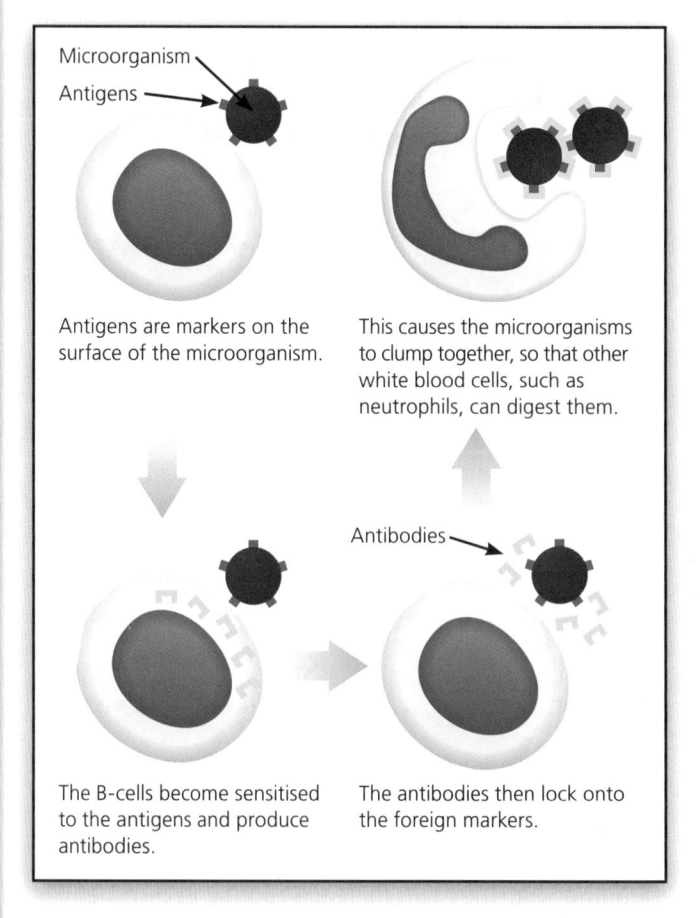

Microorganism
Antigens

Antigens are markers on the surface of the microorganism.

This causes the microorganisms to clump together, so that other white blood cells, such as neutrophils, can digest them.

Antibodies

The B-cells become sensitised to the antigens and produce antibodies.

The antibodies then lock onto the foreign markers.

The process of producing antibodies enables the immune response to be very rapid if the same microorganism infects the body again. This protects the body and gives it **immunity** against that microorganism in future.

Vaccination

Vaccination helps the body to develop long-term immunity against a disease, i.e. by producing specific antibodies. If the body is re-infected by the same microorganism, memory cells produce antibodies quickly so that the microorganism is destroyed before damage is done. This is how vaccination works:

1 Injection of vaccine

A safe form of the disease-causing microorganism is injected into the body.

2 Immune response triggered

Although the microorganism is safe, the antigens on its surface still cause the white blood cells to produce specific antibodies.

3 Memory cells remain in body

Long after the vaccination, memory cells patrol the body. If the disease-causing microorganism infects the body again, the white blood cells can attack it very quickly.

> **HT** In order to prevent an **epidemic** of a disease (like measles) in a population, it is important that as many individuals as possible are vaccinated.
>
> If more than 95% of the population is vaccinated then the unvaccinated will be protected too. This is because the risk of coming into contact with an infected person will be very small. If the percentage drops below 95%, unvaccinated individuals are more likely to get the disease and pass it on to others.
>
> If many people have the disease, the microorganism has a greater chance of mutating owing to the large number of carriers. In this case, even the vaccinated people will no longer be immune as the vaccine will be for the old form.

Risks

There is no guarantee that all vaccines and drugs (medicines) are risk free. People have genetic differences, so they may react to a vaccine or a drug in different ways. These are called **side effects**.

People always have to balance the side effects with the risk of getting the actual disease. Most side effects are minor, e.g. a mild fever or a rash.

More **extreme** side effects, e.g. encephalitis (inflammation of the brain) or convulsions, are **rare**. With the MMR (Mumps, Measles and Rubella) vaccination, the chance of getting encephalitis is 1 in 1 000 000. The risk of getting it from measles itself is between 1 in 200 and 1 in 5000 – much higher.

Some people have genes that predispose them to getting a particular side effect. For example, COX-2 Inhibitors (a type of drug used for pain relief) can cause liver damage in susceptible individuals.

Antimicrobials

Antimicrobials are chemicals that kill bacteria, fungi and viruses. An example of an antimicrobial is the metal silver, which kills bacteria.

> **HT** Antimicrobials are also used to describe chemicals that inhibit the growth of microorganisms.

Antibiotics are chemicals that are only effective against bacteria. Antibiotics are not effective against viruses, which is why you are not given them when you have the common cold or influenza.

Antimicrobial Resistance

Over a period of time, bacteria can become resistant to antimicrobials.

> **HT** Mutations (random changes) can take place in the genes of microorganisms. This leads to new strains of bacteria and fungi that are no longer affected by the antimicrobial. These reproduce and pass on the resistance. As a result, the antimicrobial is no longer effective.

To prevent resistance to antibiotics increasing:

- doctors should only prescribe them when completely necessary
- patients should always complete a course of antibiotics, even if they are feeling better.

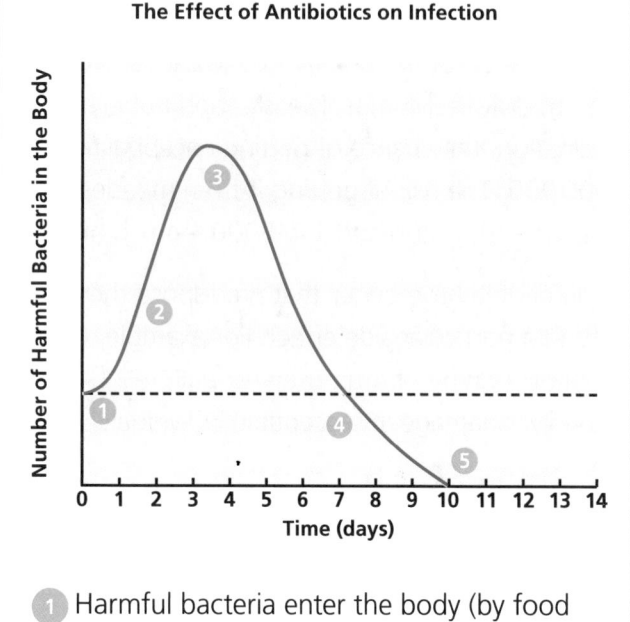

The Effect of Antibiotics on Infection

1. Harmful bacteria enter the body (by food poisoning).
2. Bacteria multiply. Patient begins to feel unwell.
3. Patient visits doctor. Starts taking antibiotics.
4. Number of bacteria now lower than originally entered the body. Patient feels better (but bacteria not all dead).
5. All harmful bacteria now destroyed.

Testing Drugs and Vaccines

Scientists are always trying to develop new drugs to fight infection. Before they can be used it is essential that the drugs are tested for **safety** and for **effectiveness**. The methods used can be controversial.

Tests on Different Types of Human Cells Grown in the Laboratory

Advantages

- Shows if drugs and vaccines are effective at targeting the problem at the cell level.
- Shows if drugs will cause damage to cells.
- No people or animals are harmed.

Disadvantages

- Does not show effects of drugs on the whole organism.
- Some people believe that growing human cells in this way is unnatural or wrong.

Tests on Animals

Advantages

- Shows if drugs are effective within body conditions.
- Shows if drugs are safe for the whole body.

Disadvantages

- Animals can suffer and die as a result of the tests.
- Animals might react differently to humans.

Following these initial tests (which can take years) **clinical trials** are carried out on **healthy volunteers** to test for safety, and on people **with the illness** to test for **safety** and **effectiveness**.

It is important to carry out long-term trials because sometimes the side effects may only become apparent after a significant period of time. Even if a drug becomes commonly issued, patients are still monitored to check that it is still safe. The drug can be withdrawn if the benefits no longer outweigh the risks.

Clinical trials normally compare the effects of new drugs to old ones. They have to be carefully planned to ensure the results are as accurate and reliable as possible. Patients have to agree to be part of a trial.

There are three types of trial:

1 Open-label Trial

An open-label trial is where both the doctor and patient know that they are using a new treatment. This is used when the new treatment is very similar to the original, or when a drug is being compared to physical therapy.

2 Blind Trial

A blind trial is where the doctor knows which treatment (i.e. the treatment or the control) the patient is receiving, but the patient does not. The idea is to remove bias – the patient may give biased information if they know which treatment is being given. An example would be using a new type of surgery on a patient.

3 Double-blind Trial

A double-blind trial is where neither the patient nor the doctor administering the treatment knows whether the patient is receiving the treatment or the control. This removes the possibility of both the doctors and the patients introducing any bias.

The most rigorous trial is the double-blind trial. However, sometimes it is impossible to stop a patient or doctor from realising what treatment is being given, e.g. if the new drug has a different taste or has physical effects on the body.

Placebos

Placebos (dummy drugs containing no medication) are occasionally used in medical trials. However, they are not common practice because they create an **ethical dilemma**.

Trials involving placebos benefit society because they help to establish whether a new drug is effective or not. However, when doctors give sick patients a placebo rather than the real treatment they are offering them **false hope**. The patient believes that the pill will cure them but the doctor knows it will not.

It is also difficult to disguise a placebo. If a new drug is expected to produce certain side effects and the patient does not display them, they may work out that a placebo has been given.

For example, if a diuretic (a drug increasing urine production) is being tested, it would be easy to work out which patient had received the placebo.

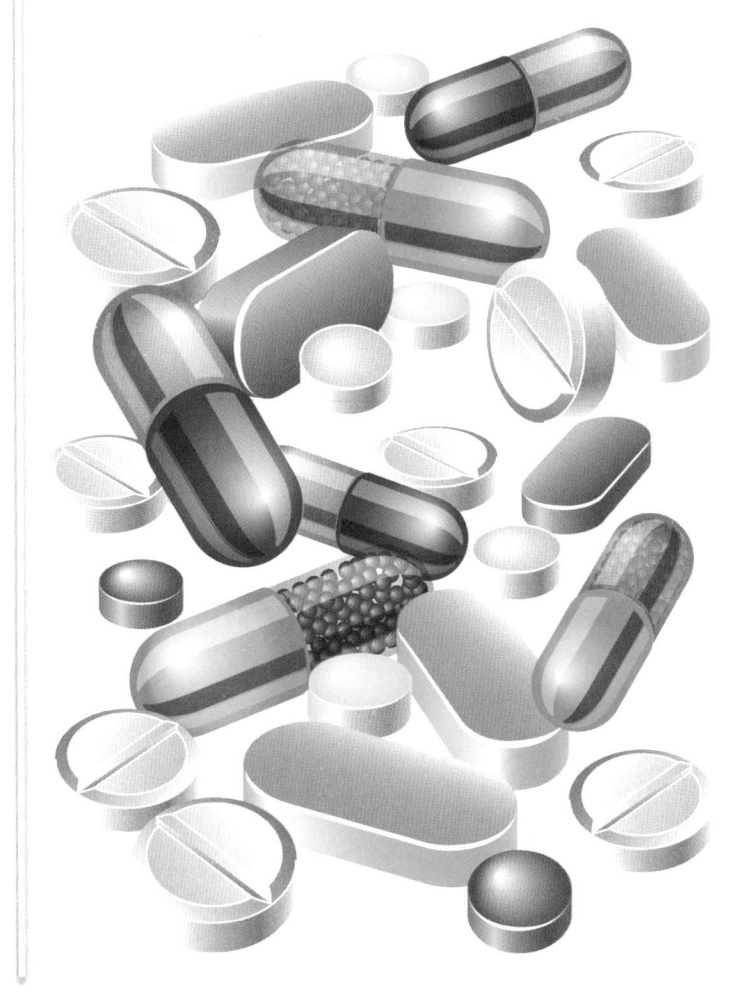

The Heart

The heart is a muscular organ in the circulatory system. It beats automatically, pumping blood around the body to provide cells with oxygen and dissolved food for **respiration**. The blood removes carbon dioxide and water as waste products.

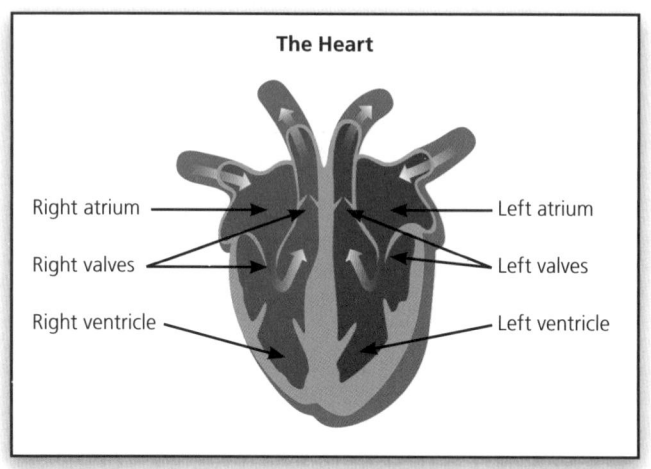

The Heart

Right atrium
Right valves
Right ventricle
Left atrium
Left valves
Left ventricle

Blood from the rest of the body enters the right atrium of the heart. It then moves into the right ventricle before being pumped to the lungs. When the oxygenated blood returns to the heart, it enters the left atrium. It then moves into the left ventricle before being pumped to the rest of the body. The heart is called a **double pump** because blood returns to it twice.

The heart itself is mainly made up of muscle cells. These cells also require oxygen and dissolved food, so the heart needs its own blood supply.

Arteries, Veins and Capillaries

Arteries carry blood away from the heart **towards** the organs. Substances cannot pass through the artery walls.

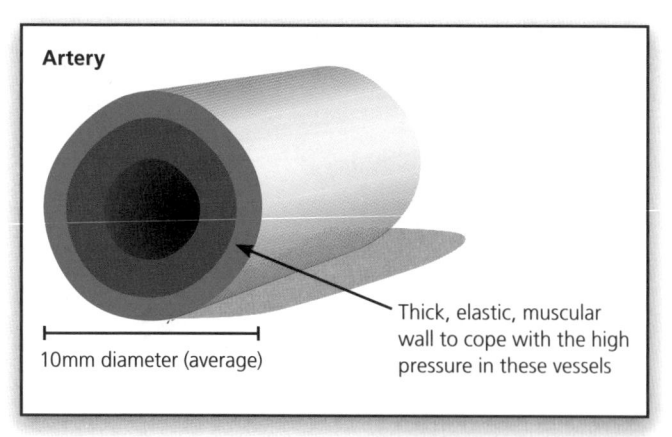

Artery

Thick, elastic, muscular wall to cope with the high pressure in these vessels

10mm diameter (average)

Veins carry blood from the organs back to the heart. Substances cannot pass through the walls of a vein.

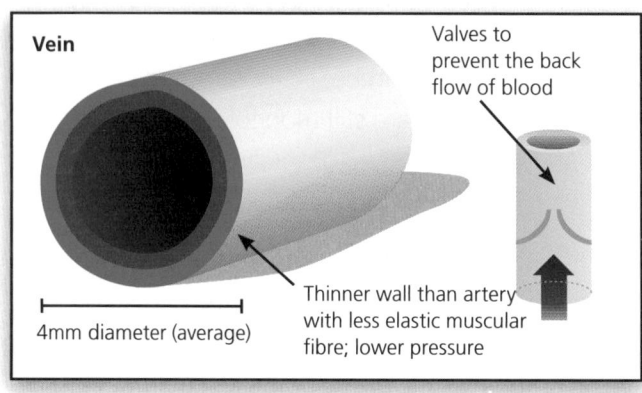

Vein

Valves to prevent the back flow of blood

Thinner wall than artery with less elastic muscular fibre; lower pressure

4mm diameter (average)

Capillaries are narrow, thin-walled vessels that allow blood to move through one cell at a time. Dissolved gases and nutrients can move out of the capillary into the surrounding cells. Waste products move back into the blood.

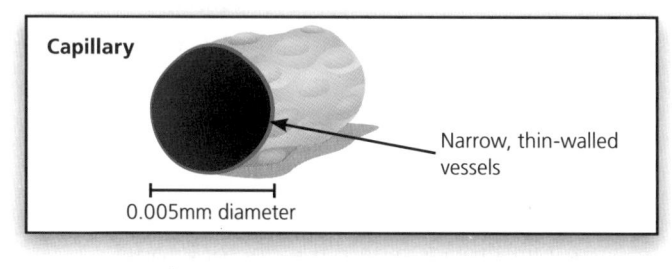

Capillary

Narrow, thin-walled vessels

0.005mm diameter

Heart Disease

Heart disease is an abnormality of the heart that can lead to a **heart attack**. It is usually caused by **lifestyle** and / or **genetic factors**, not by infection by microorganisms. Lifestyle factors that can lead to heart disease include:

- poor diet
- cigarette smoking
- misuse of drugs (e.g. alcohol, nicotine, Ecstasy, cannabis)
- stress.

Fatty deposits can build up in the blood vessels supplying the heart. This restricts the blood flow and the muscle cells do not get enough oxygen and nutrients. This can cause a heart attack.

Heart disease is more common in the UK than in non-industrialised countries. This is probably because people in the UK tend to be less active and the typical diet in the UK is high in salt and fats.

Reducing the Risk

There are precautions people can take to reduce the risk of heart disease. One of the easiest is to exercise regularly with the aim of raising the heart rate without putting it under too much stress, e.g. 20 minutes of brisk walking every day.

Health professionals can use information about a person's lifestyle, together with genetic data (family history and genetic tests), to give an indication of how likely that person is to suffer from heart disease. If the risk is high then steps, such as those listed below, can be taken to reduce the risk of heart failure:

* Do not smoke.
* Reduce salt intake in the diet.
* Maintain a healthy body weight.
* Monitor cholesterol levels (and use cholesterol-reducing drugs and foods if necessary).

Testing the Heart

The heart rate can be measured by taking the pulse. If it is too fast or slow, then it could indicate problems. Misusing drugs (such as Ecstasy, cannabis, nicotine and alcohol) can cause negative effects on health. These include altering the heart rate and blood pressure. The risk of suffering a heart attack increases.

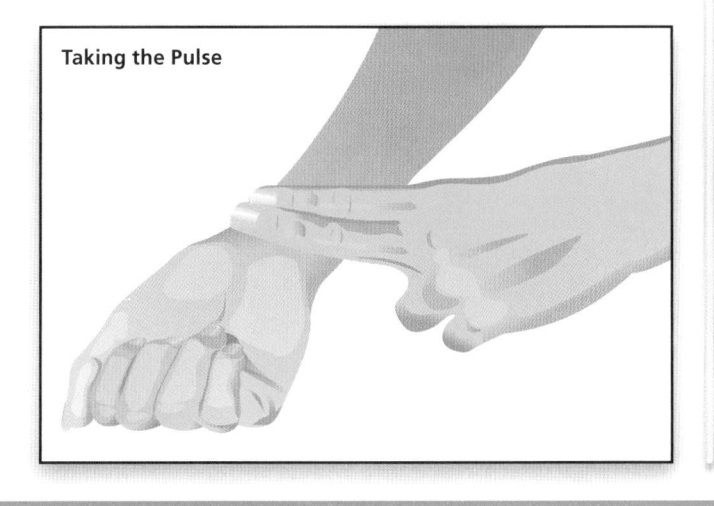

Taking the Pulse

Blood pressure is the pressure of the blood against the walls of the arteries and it results from two forces:

* **Systolic** pressure from the heart as it contracts and pumps blood into the arteries and through the circulatory system.
* **Diastolic** pressure from the force of the arteries as they resist the flow when the heart relaxes.

The pressure of the blood against the walls of the arteries can also be measured using a **sphygmomanometer**.

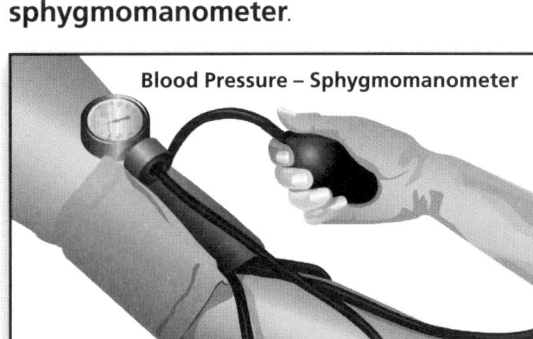
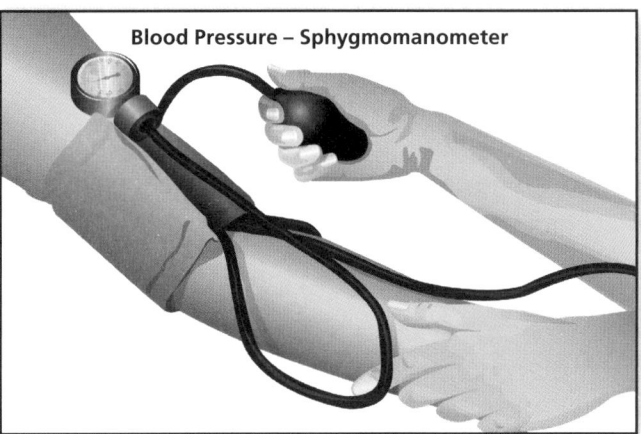

Blood Pressure – Sphygmomanometer

The sphygmomanometer gives two numbers and gives the force needed to move the metal mercury inside (hence the unit is **mmHg**):

The numbers are reported as a fraction, e.g. 118 over 76 means the systolic pressure is 118 mmHg and diastolic pressure is 76 mmHg. An average blood pressure reading is 128/80 mmHg.

A high blood pressure reading increases the chance of heart disease. 'Normal' measurements for pulse and blood pressure are always given as ranges. This is because people are not identical.

Studying Heart Disease

As heart disease is a big killer worldwide, studies continue to try to identify what factors cause it. These are called epidemiological studies and they try to identify whether a factor present in a large number of sufferers is the cause. In addition, there are more and more genetic studies taking place to identify the genes responsible for heart disease.

Homeostasis

Homeostasis is the maintenance of a constant internal environment. It is achieved by balancing bodily inputs and outputs, using the nervous system and hormones to control the process.

The body has automatic control systems which ensure that the correct, steady levels of different factors, e.g. temperature and water, are maintained. These factors are important for cells to be able to function properly.

For homeostasis to work, these control systems need to have:

- receptors (sensors) to detect changes in the environment
- processing centres to receive information and coordinate responses automatically
- effectors that produce the response.

Negative Feedback

When receptors detect that the temperature in the body has increased above a certain level, the processing centre (the brain) sends signals to the effectors (in this case sweat glands) to produce sweat to cool down the body. This process, where the steady state of the body is adjusted to reverse the change, is called **negative feedback**.

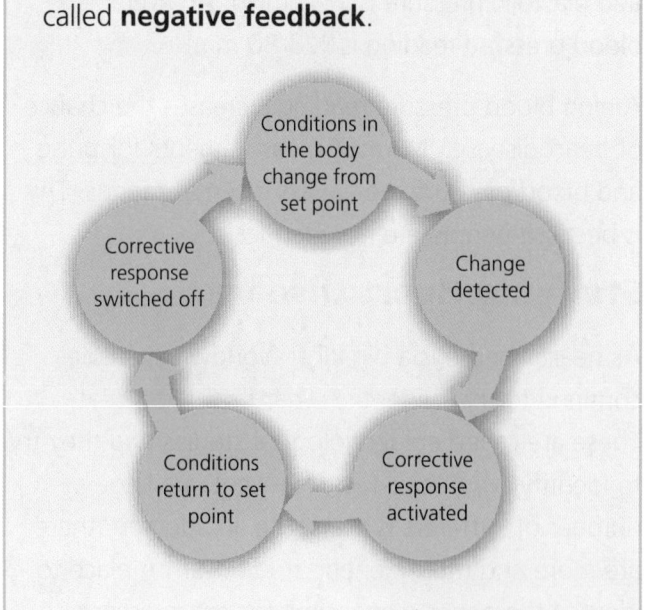

Water Balance

Water is input (gained) from drinks, food and respiration. It is output (lost) through sweating, breathing and the excretion of faeces and urine. The body has to balance these different inputs and outputs to ensure that there is enough water inside cells for cell activity to take place.

Most people have two kidneys, one situated on either side of the spine on the back wall of the abdomen. It is the job of the kidneys to control the balance of water in the body. This is achieved by adjusting the amount of urine that is excreted from the body.

The kidneys filter the blood to remove all waste (urea) and to balance levels of other chemicals (including water). The body achieves this balance through several stages:

1. Filtering small molecules from the blood to form urine (water, salt and urea).
2. Reabsorbing all the sugar for respiration.
3. Reabsorbing as much salt as the body requires.
4. Reabsorbing as much water as the body requires.
5. Excreting the remaining urine, which is stored in the bladder.

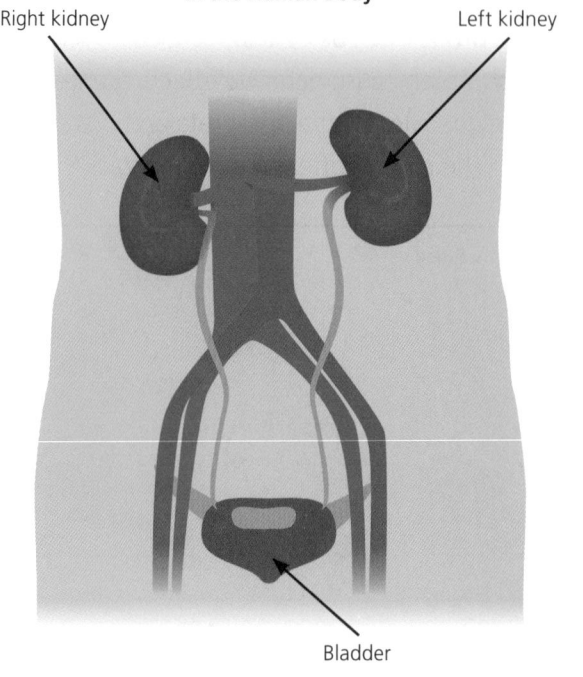

Location of the Kidneys and Bladder in the Human Body

The brain monitors water content constantly and causes the kidneys to adjust the concentration and volume of urine produced.

If the water level in the body is too low, more water is reabsorbed by the kidneys. If the water level is too high, the urine becomes more dilute and watery.

The amount of water that needs to be reabsorbed depends on a number of factors:

- **External temperature**

  High ➤ concentrated urine

  Low ➤ dilute urine

- **Level of exercise**

  High ➤ concentrated urine

  Low ➤ dilute urine

- **Fluid intake**

  High ➤ dilute urine

  Low ➤ concentrated urine

- **Salt intake**

  High ➤ dilute urine

  Low ➤ concentrated urine

> **HT** The concentration of urine is controlled by a hormone called **ADH**, which is released into the bloodstream by the **pituitary gland**.
>
> When the level of water in the blood is too low, ADH is released and this causes concentrated urine to be produced. This is because the hormone causes the kidney to become more permeable, allowing water to be reabsorbed.
>
> When the level of water in the blood is too high, ADH is not released. The kidney becomes less permeable and this causes dilute, watery urine to be produced.
>
> This is another example of negative feedback.

Effect of Alcohol

Alcohol is a drug that causes the production of a greater volume of dilute, watery urine. This can lead to dehydration and other adverse effects on health. The symptoms of dehydration include headaches, which, unsurprisingly, are also a symptom of hangovers.

> **HT** The reason why alcohol leads to the production of greater volumes of urine is because ADH is suppressed.

Effect of Ecstasy

Ecstasy is a drug that makes people feel euphoric. It can increase the heart rate and blood pressure, which can cause long-term health problems, including increasing the chance of having a heart attack.

The drug also interferes with the brain, causing errors in monitoring the water content of the body. Although someone taking Ecstasy may get hot and drink a lot of water, the brain fails to send messages to the kidneys to get rid of the extra water.

The urine that is produced is concentrated when it should be dilute. As the water cannot escape, it causes cells to swell up. Cells in the brain get squashed against the skull and die. This may result in death.

> **HT** The reason why Ecstasy leads to the retention of greater volumes of water is because it causes increased ADH production.

Effects of Cannabis and Nicotine

Cannabis and nicotine are drugs that are smoked. They have the effect of increasing the heart rate. Cannabis reduces blood pressure whilst nicotine increases it. These effects can cause long-term heart problems and increase the risk of a heart attack.

All life on Earth is adapted for living in particular habitats. This module looks at:

- how living things are adapted to the environment
- how nutrients such as carbon and nitrogen are cycled
- how life evolved
- the evidence for evolution.

Adaptations

A group of organisms that can breed together and produce fertile offspring is called a **species**.

The individuals in a species are adapted to living in their environment. This means that their features work best with the environment that they live in. For example, polar bears are adapted to living in the Arctic and tigers are adapted to the jungle.

All living things rely on their environment and other species to survive. A **habitat** is the term used to describe the environment in which an animal or plant lives.

The adaptation of living organisms to their environment enables the organisms to live longer. If an organism survives to sexual maturity, it is more likely to pass on its genes, including the genes coding for its adaptations, to the next generation. Adaptations therefore can lead to increased chances of survival.

When the same **resources** (e.g. shelter, food, water, light availability, etc.) are needed by different organisms in the same habitat then there is **competition**. The organisms that are most successful at competing survive and pass on those genes that code for the adaptations.

Cactus

The cactus is a plant native to America that is supremely adapted for living in conditions of high temperature and low rainfall.

A cactus plant has the following adaptations that enable it to survive in the environment that it lives in.

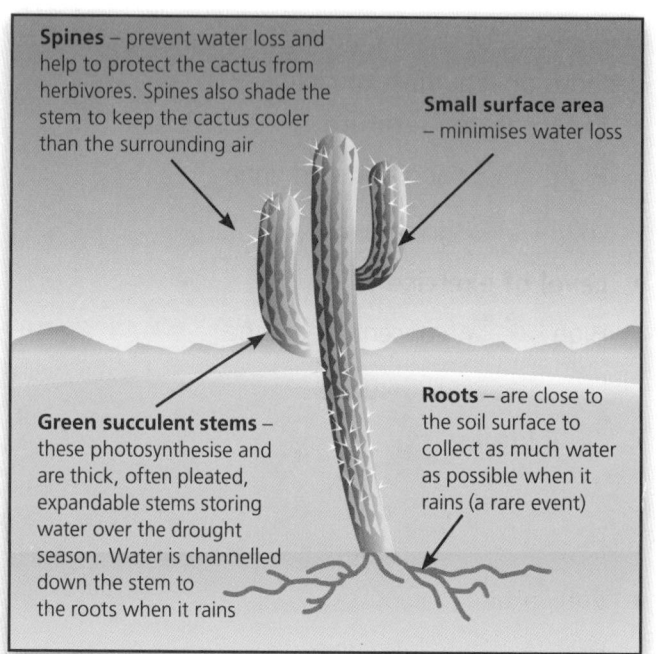

Spines – prevent water loss and help to protect the cactus from herbivores. Spines also shade the stem to keep the cactus cooler than the surrounding air

Small surface area – minimises water loss

Green succulent stems – these photosynthesise and are thick, often pleated, expandable stems storing water over the drought season. Water is channelled down the stem to the roots when it rains

Roots – are close to the soil surface to collect as much water as possible when it rains (a rare event)

Cacti are typically found in hot, dry climates. Their adaptations enable them to survive and pass on their successful genes to the next generation.

The table shows the number of cacti per km² in different areas of North America.

US State	Average August Temperature (°C)	Number of Cacti per km²
Texas	23.6	100
N. Mexico	24	120
California	21	70
Alaska	16	0

Looking at the table, we could explain that cacti are found in hot climates because their adaptations (spines, green succulent stems, roots close to the surface and small surface area) enable them to survive where other plants cannot.

They do not do well in colder climates, such as in Alaska, because their adaptations are not suited to colder climates.

Food Chains and Food Webs

Food chains show the direction of energy and material transfer between organisms.

Food webs show how all the food chains in a given habitat are interrelated. In practice, these can be very complex because many animals have varied diets. All the organisms in a food web are dependent on other parts of the web.

> **HT** This is called **interdependence**.

A Food Web

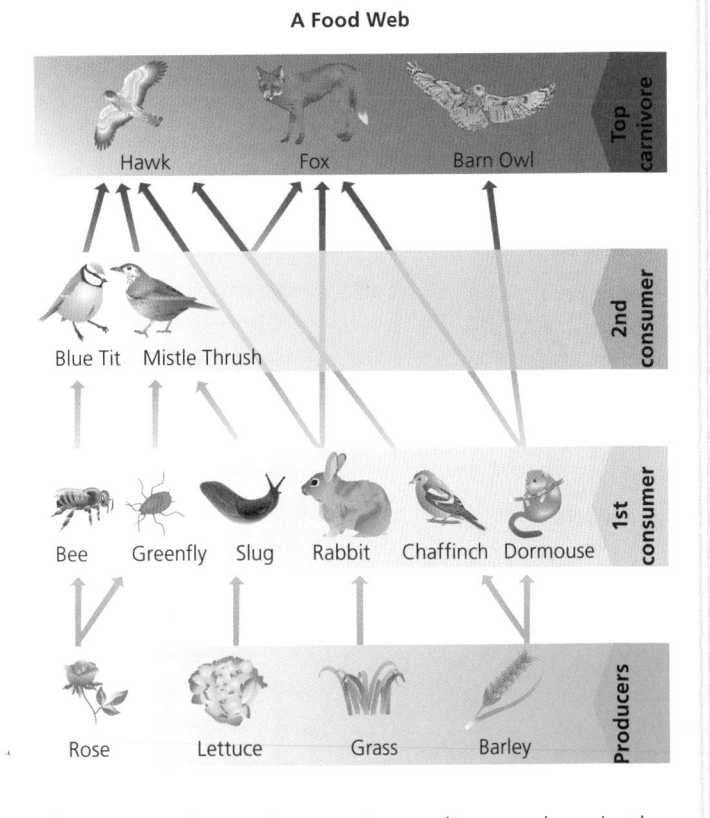

Changes to the environment can alter numbers in the food web. For example, a small decrease in the amount of rain could reduce the amount of lettuce available and cause reductions in the number of slugs.

If the changes are too great for the natural variation within a population to cope with, then organisms will die out before they can reproduce. The population will decline and eventually become extinct (disappear completely).

The same process happens if a new species that is better at competing for resources (a competitor) is introduced. A new predator or a disease organism for a species can have the same effect.

If a species (animal, plant or microorganism) becomes extinct, this can affect other parts of the food web and cause further extinctions.

Energy Flow Through Food Chains

Energy from the Sun enters the food chain when green plants absorb light in order to photosynthesise. When animals eat the plants, the energy passes up the food chain from one organism to another.

Energy in a food chain flows in one direction:

1. A small proportion of the Sun's light energy transfers to an **autotroph** (a plant), which captures the energy, carries out photosynthesis and stores the energy in chemicals (such as cellulose) in its cells.
2. A **herbivore heterotroph** then eats the autotroph. Some of the energy stored in the plant is transferred to the herbivore and stored in its cells.
3. A **carnivore heterotroph** then eats the herbivore heterotroph. Some of the energy stored in the herbivore is transferred to the carnivore and stored in its cells.

Energy Flow in a Food Chain

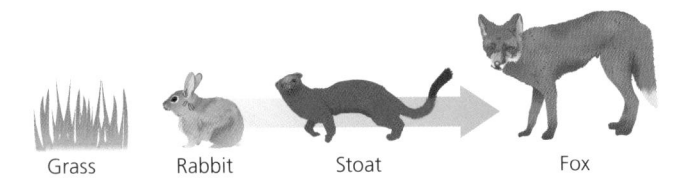

Grass   Rabbit   Stoat   Fox

At each stage of the food chain, a large proportion of the energy is:

- lost to the environment as heat
- excreted as waste products
- trapped in indigestible material such as bones, cellulose and fur.

This means that as the food chain moves from autotrophs to heterotrophs, there is less energy available at each **trophic level** (i.e. each stage of the food chain). Therefore there is a limit to the number of levels in each food chain. The limit is usually four or five levels.

Decay Organisms

Energy is also transferred by decay organisms that break down organisms after they die.

There are two types of decay organism:

- **Decomposers**, such as bacteria and fungi, break down the dead material and use the energy stored inside.

- **Detritivores** include animals such as earthworms and woodlice. These consume the detritus (dead plants or animals and their waste), breaking it down into smaller particles that other detritivores and decomposers can use.

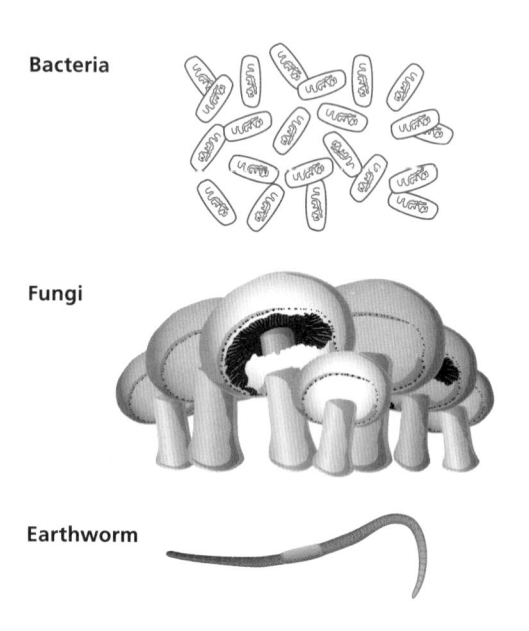

Bacteria

Fungi

Earthworm

Calculating Energy Efficiency

The percentage of energy efficiency can be calculated using the following formula:

$$\text{Percentage of energy successfully transferred} = \frac{\text{Amount used}}{\text{Amount potentially available}} \times 100$$

Example

The arrow diagram to the right shows the feeding relationship between a green plant, a caterpillar and a bird.

Calculate how efficient the energy transfer is for the caterpillar feeding on the plant.

$$\text{Percentage of energy successfully transferred} = \frac{\text{Amount used}}{\text{Amount potentially available}} \times 100$$

$$= \frac{80}{800} \times 100$$

$$= \textbf{10\%}$$

On average, only 10% of the energy from the Sun ends up being stored as plant tissue. If an animal eats a plant, 10% of the energy gained is used to build up biomass. The rest of the energy is used by the animal to respire, move and keep warm.

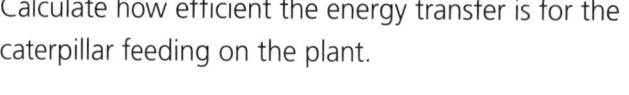

Bird

15

65 Energy lost

Caterpillar
80

720 Energy lost

800 units of energy in plant

Carbon

Carbon is a vital element for living things. It is used in all organic molecules, including sugars, proteins and amino acids. Life on Earth is very much carbon-based.

Carbon is recycled through the environment so that it is available for life processes. This can be seen in the **carbon cycle**:

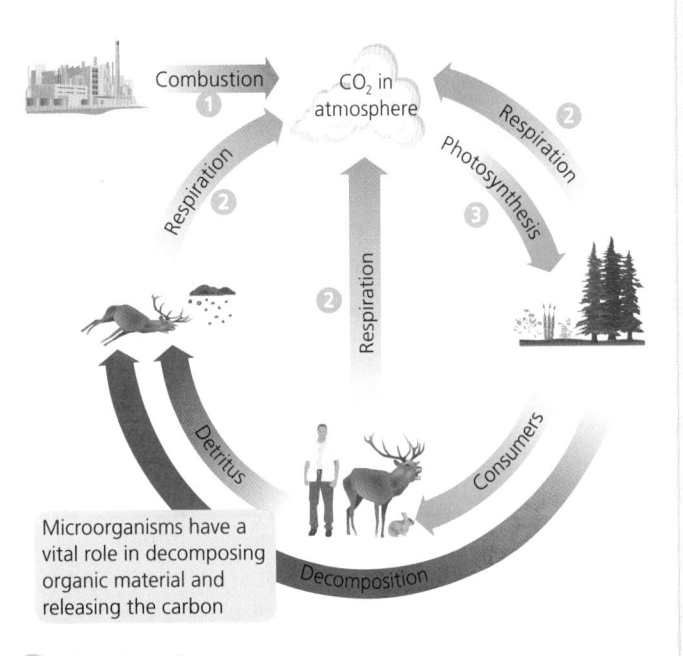

Microorganisms have a vital role in decomposing organic material and releasing the carbon

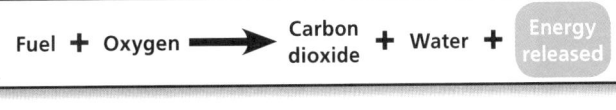

1 Combustion

Fuel + Oxygen ⟶ Carbon dioxide + Water + Energy released

2 Respiration

Glucose + Oxygen ⟶ Carbon dioxide + Water + Energy released

3 Photosynthesis

Carbon dioxide + Water ⟶(Light energy) Glucose + Oxygen

Nitrogen

Another element vital for life is nitrogen. Nitrogen gas makes up 79% of the Earth's atmosphere. Nitrogen molecules have a triple covalent bond between the atoms of nitrogen and this makes it impossible for most organisms to break the bond and use the nitrogen.

Nitrogen is 'fixed' into a form that plants and animals can use in two ways: lightning strikes and the action of specialised bacteria.

Nitrogen, like carbon, has to be recycled to ensure that it is available for life processes. This can be seen in the **nitrogen cycle**:

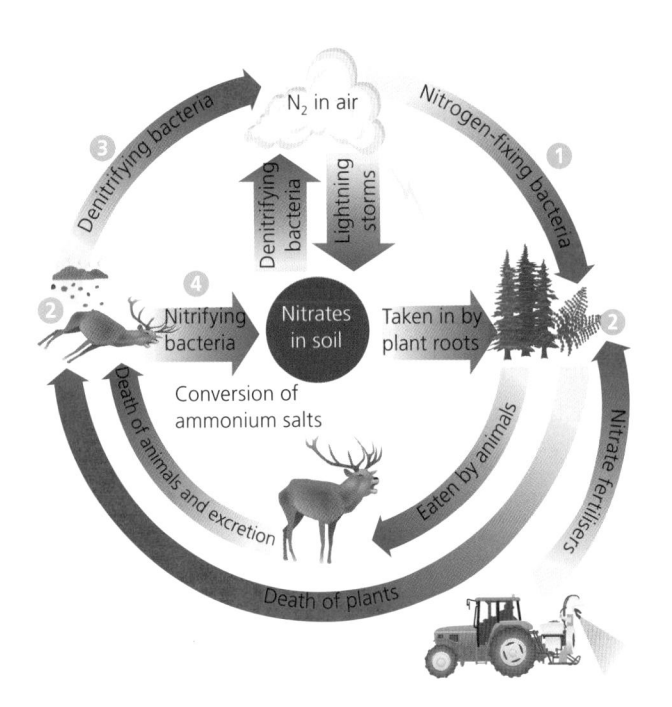

HT 1 Nitrogen fixation – carried out by bacteria such as *Azotobacter sp.* and blue green algae such as *Anabaena variabilis*

2 Conversion of nitrogen compounds into proteins inside plants and animals

3 Denitrification – this is where, in the absence of oxygen, denitrifying bacteria such as *Thiobacillus denitrificans* convert nitrates in dead plants and animal remains back into nitrogen gas. This completes the cycle, releasing nitrogen back into the atmosphere.

4 Microorganisms convert ammonia to nitrites and then to nitrates via the process of nitrification.

The nitrogen that is now in compounds in plant material is passed through the food chain through animals eating the plants.

Measuring Environmental Changes

Biologists can measure changes in the environment by using indicators. These may be non-living or living.

Non-living Indicators

Nitrate levels can be measured using test kits with chemicals that change colour. The chemicals can then be matched against a chart indicating the amount of nitrate present in the sample.

Temperature can be measured using a thermometer, or a data-logger, which is more accurate and reliable.

Carbon dioxide levels can be measured using data-loggers.

Biological Indicators

Changes in the environment affect living organisms. Biologists can use changes in the pattern of where a species is living to determine how climate change or other environmental changes, such as road-building projects, are affecting the species.

In the oceans, **phytoplankton** (microscopic plants) are useful for detecting the effect of temperature changes and for detecting changes in the food web.

Lichens grow very slowly and are susceptible to atmospheric pollutants and acid rain. A decline in their number can indicate pollution.

River organisms, such as the larvae of mayfly (called **mayfly nymphs**), can be used to indicate the quality of the water. Mayfly nymphs can only live in clean river water with enough oxygen. If a river has mayfly nymphs, then pollution levels will be low.

River pollution typically causes mass growth of bacteria, which then use up all the oxygen. This causes fish to die and indicator species such as **bloodworm** and **rat-tailed maggots** to grow instead, as these are pollution tolerant and can survive in low oxygen concentrations.

Biological Indicators in a River

Direction of water flow

Location	Species Present	Number of Individuals (m³)
A	Mayfly nymph	113
	Trout	2
	Stonefly nymph	84
B	Bloodworm	25
	Rat-tailed maggot	46
C	Caddisfly larvae	45
	Freshwater shrimp	59
D	Mayfly nymph	89
	Freshwater shrimp	90

The evidence suggests that the factory is polluting the river due to the change in indicator species present.

How Life Evolved

Life on Earth began around 3500 million years ago. **All** life on Earth, including all life that is now extinct, evolved from very simple living things. So all organisms share a common ancestor.

The naturalist Charles Darwin thought creatively about the problem of how organisms are related. Creative thinking is a skill scientists need when developing explanations. To show the linked ancestors of different species, he drew a tree of life to illustrate his thinking:

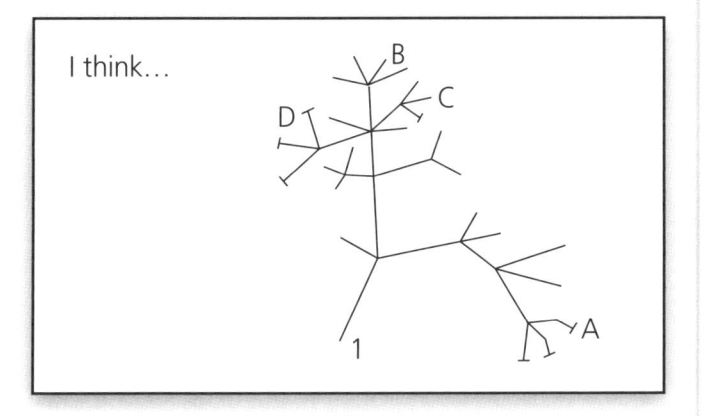

The evidence of the fact that organisms share a common ancestor comes from:

1 The Fossil Record

Fossils are the remains of plants or animals from thousands of years ago that are found in rock. Fossils indicate the history of species and can show the evolutionary changes in organisms over millions of years. Fossils can be formed from the hard parts of animals that did not decay easily, or from parts of plants or animals that did not decay

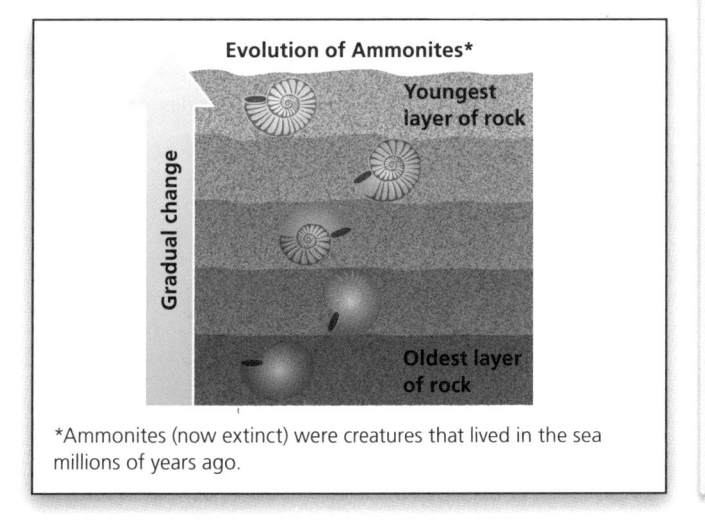

Evolution of Ammonites*

Youngest layer of rock

Gradual change

Oldest layer of rock

*Ammonites (now extinct) were creatures that lived in the sea millions of years ago.

because one or more of the conditions needed for decay were absent, e.g. oxygen, moisture and temperature. The remains of the organisms are then buried until they are rediscovered.

2 Genomics

Similarities and differences in DNA can lead to the relationships being worked out between all life on Earth. Analysing the DNA of both living and fossilised specimens shows that there are similarities as well as differences. This can be used to chart the family tree of all life on Earth. The more shared genes organisms have, the more closely related they are.

Mapping the differences and similarities enables the family relationships between organisms to be measured. For example, the diagram below (a **phylogenetic tree**) shows the relationship between the different genes for mouse taste receptors (blue) and the taste receptors in humans (gold). The red markers indicate where the taste receptor is the same in mice and humans. We share 11 taste receptors with mice and approximately 85% of all our genes.

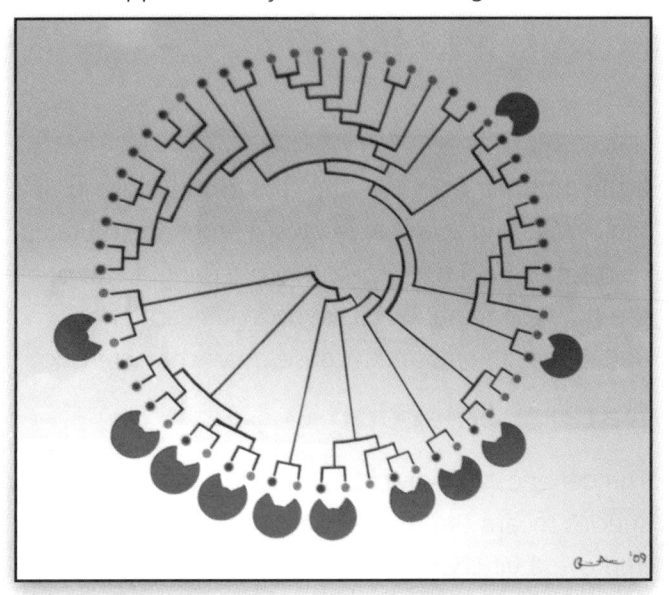

All organisms have DNA. Organisms in a species differ from one another, e.g. offspring look different to their parents. These changes are due to the environment and genetic differences in the DNA. Only the **changes** in DNA (mutations) can be passed on to the offspring.

Gene Mutation

Genetic variation is caused when changes called **mutations** take place in the genes. Mutations cause different proteins to be produced and this changes the function of the gene. Sometimes a mutation causes a gene to be copied twice, which means that more variation can occur.

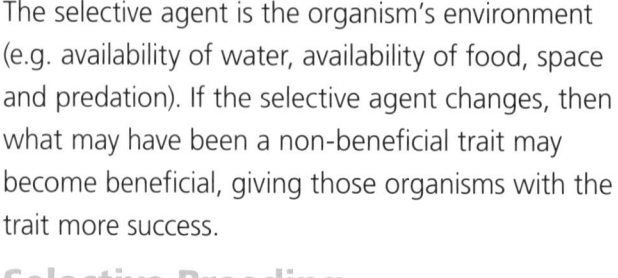

Example of a Gene Mutation

These three bases produce the amino acid cysteine

T G C

This base has mutated so now the amino acid tyrosine is produced

T A

If the mutations occur in the cells producing eggs in the ovaries and sperm in the testes, then the mutated genes may be passed on to the offspring. Most of the time the mutations have no significant effect. Sometimes the mutation causes new characteristics.

Natural Selection

The genetic variation between individuals in a species means that those with characteristics that improve their chances of survival in their physical environment are more likely to live to adulthood.

When these individuals reproduce, they pass on the beneficial characteristics to their offspring. Individuals with characteristics poorly-fitting to their environment are less likely to survive.

As a result, the number of individuals in a population with beneficial traits increases while the number of individuals with non-beneficial traits decreases.

The selective agent is the organism's environment (e.g. availability of water, availability of food, space and predation). If the selective agent changes, then what may have been a non-beneficial trait may become beneficial, giving those organisms with the trait more success.

Selective Breeding

Selective breeding is where animals and plants with certain traits are deliberately mated together (crossed) to produce offspring with certain desirable characteristics.

① Creating New Varieties of Organisms

Dalmation Dogs

Choose the spottiest two to breed…

… and then the spottiest of their offspring…

… to eventually get Dalmations.

2 Increasing the Yield of Animals and Plants

Some types of cattle have been bred to produce high yields of milk, or milk with a low fat content.

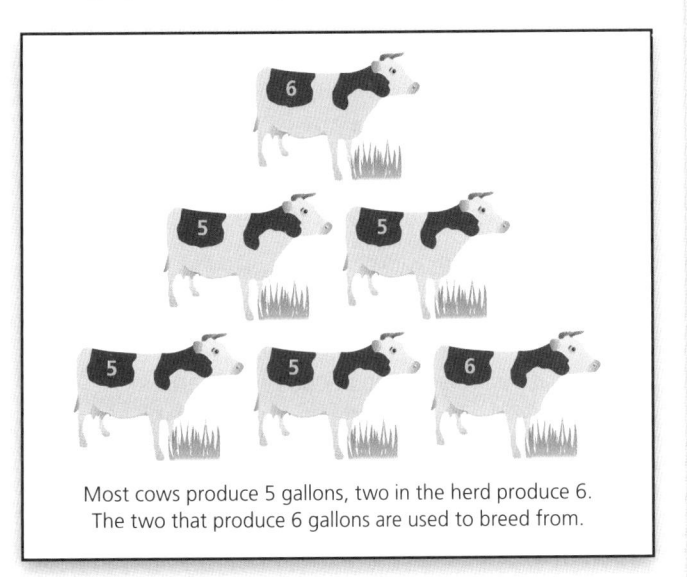

Most cows produce 5 gallons, two in the herd produce 6.
The two that produce 6 gallons are used to breed from.

Improved crops can be obtained through selective breeding programmes, although this happens over a long period of time.

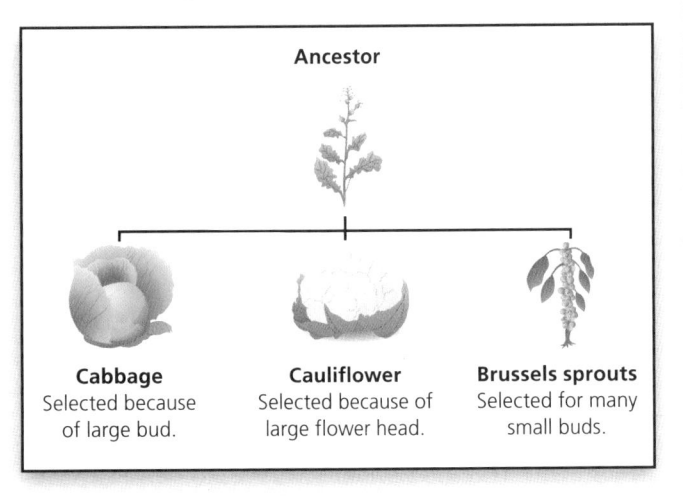

Ancestor

Cabbage	**Cauliflower**	**Brussels sprouts**
Selected because of large bud.	Selected because of large flower head.	Selected for many small buds.

Natural Selection and Selective Breeding – Differences and Similarities

Differences
With selective breeding, it is humans who choose the desirable traits. With natural selection, it is the environment that determines the desirable traits.

Similarities
Both natural selection and selective breeding act on the genetic variation within a population.

Peppered Moths

Peppered moths are usually pale and speckled in colour. This means that they are well-camouflaged against the bark of silver birch trees.

Within the population is a trait that causes the moth to be completely black. The black moths are at a disadvantage because predators can see them more easily against the tree. When pollution from factories covered the trees with black soot, the situation was reversed.

The Clean Air Act in the 1950s caused the amount of pollution to decrease drastically:

Numbers of Peppered Moths Caught in a Day		
Data from 1900		
	Black	**Speckled**
Industrial	135	29
Countryside	5	180
Data from 2000		
	Black	**Speckled**
Industrial	9	160
Countryside	7	171

Conclusion: the coloration of the moth was selected for by the environmental conditions.

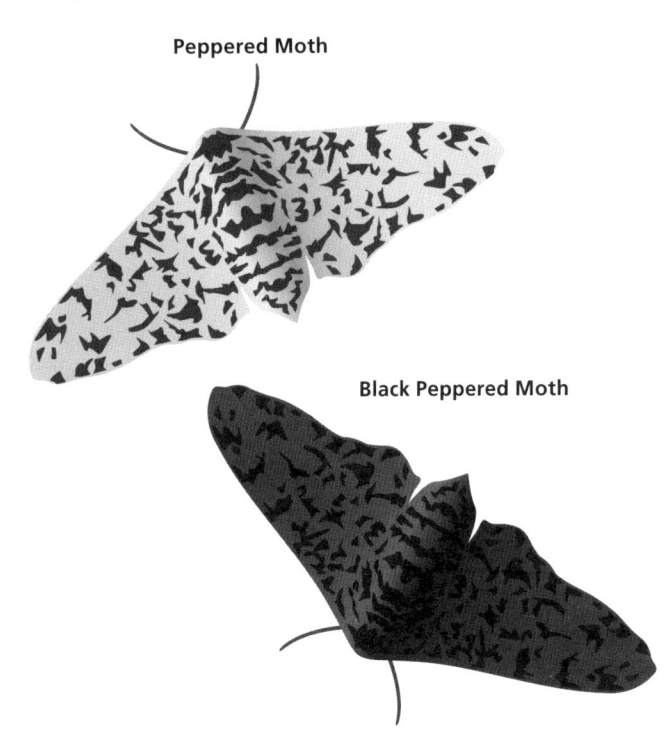

Peppered Moth

Black Peppered Moth

Evolution

The combined effects of the following can lead to the formation of new species:

- Mutations
- Natural selection
- Environmental changes
- Isolation – where individuals from one population are isolated from other populations so that they cannot meet to breed.

This process is called **evolution**.

Jean-Baptiste Lamarck was a scientist who proposed that the environment changed an organism. The organism then passed on the characteristic to their offspring, e.g. moles lived in the dark, so they lost their eyes as a result. This is called **evolution through inheritance of acquired characteristics**.

Charles Darwin devised a better explanation following many years of thought and collecting evidence. By collecting data, Darwin made the connection between varieties, competition, the survival of the fittest and the passing on of desirable characteristics to the next generation.

This is an example of how the science community works. Darwin had come up with a scientific explanation that was better than previous explanations, such as Lamarck's. It fitted the available evidence at the time, and it fits with our modern understanding of genetics today. There was, however, no evidence or scientific mechanism for Lamarck's inheritance of acquired characteristics. The scientific community, having repeated Darwin's experiments and peer reviewed his work, accepts Darwin's explanation for evolution over Lamarck's.

Today it is accepted that **all** life on Earth arose through the process of **evolution through natural selection**.

Biodiversity

Biodiversity refers to the variety of life on Earth. It can be measured in a number of ways:

- The number of different species present in an area
- The range of different types of organism (e.g. plants, animals and microorganisms)
- The genetic variation within species (how many different alleles there are).

The greater these are, the greater the biodiversity.

Biodiversity is important because it enables ecosystems and the species within them to survive natural disasters. For humans it is vitally important because we need to exploit crops to feed a growing population. Plants are also the source of compounds that are effective against disease and genetic disorders. These could potentially be used as medicines. For example, quinine, a drug effective against malaria, was discovered and extracted from the quinchona tree in South America.

If ecosystems are destroyed and biodiversity is reduced, then drugs and food substances may be lost for future generations.

Classification

All life on Earth can be divided into groups based on similarities and differences in their physical features (e.g. flowers in flowering plants, the skeleton in vertebrates) and in their DNA.

The groups start off large with high numbers of organisms with a few features in common (e.g. **Kingdoms** such as plants, animals) and reduce in size as they are sub-divided into much smaller groups containing organisms with similar features (e.g. **species** such as *Homo sapiens*).

Classifying both living and fossil organisms can help to make sense of the enormous diversity of living things on Earth as well as to show the evolutionary relationships between organisms.

Extinction

Throughout the history of Earth, species of animals and plants have become extinct (i.e they do not exist anywhere on the planet), e.g. the dodo.

The rate of extinctions on Earth has been increasing. This is likely to be due to human activity. Humans can cause extinctions directly or indirectly:

Direct Causes
• Excessive hunting of animals
• Removal of habitats to extract resources (e.g. timber from rainforests) or for building

Indirect Causes
• Introducing predators to new locations (e.g. when colonising Australia)
• Activities causing global warming – the activities of humans indirectly change the environmental conditions
• Trying to eradicate a pest – this can have a knock-on effect on other members of a food web

Sustainability

Sustainability is about meeting the needs of people today without damaging the Earth for future generations.

Farming

In the past, farmers used to grow a variety of different crops on a smallholding. Hedgerows would separate the different parts of the farm. In the 20th century, techniques changed. Giant fields made from many earlier fields joined together were planted with **monocultures** (a single variety of a crop).

This change to intensive farming has advantages because it maximises the amount of food available for the population. However, it reduces biodiversity. Hedgerows have decreased in number and the food chains that rely on them have also decreased. Intensive farming is not sustainable because it does not maintain biodiversity.

However, the solution is not to revert to old-fashioned methods of farming. To ensure all people can have food, scientists need to work out new ways of optimising intensive farming while maximising sustainability.

Improving Sustainability

Virtually all products used in the industrialised world rely on oil and the products made from it. To improve sustainability, alternatives to oil need to be found.

Packaging is used to attract the attention of consumers, as well as providing a way of keeping the product safe. Packaging is often made from oil-based plastics.

Manufacturers have to consider:
- what **materials** should be used
- how much **energy** is needed in the manufacturing process for a given packaging material
- how much **pollution** will be produced as a result of manufacturing packaging.

For example, crude oil is a fossil fuel that takes millions of years to form and the plastic that is made from oil will not biodegrade. Using oil is therefore unsustainable, as it cannot be remade.

Sustainable alternatives would include using a packet made from paper or from cellulose-based plastics. The type of plants that produced the material can then be re-planted.

Packaging ends up being thrown away. The rubbish is taken to **landfill** sites. Even if the packaging is biodegradable, there will still be slow decomposition as there is a lack of oxygen in landfill.

Manufacturing and transporting packaging also use up energy and produce pollution. It would therefore be far more preferable to reduce the amount of packaging used for products.

For example, Easter eggs are sold in bright boxes with a plastic insert (made from oil) to display the egg, which is encased in foil. Some companies are now selling eco-friendly Easter eggs. These consist of just the egg wrapped in paper or foil. This reduces the waste, pollution and energy costs for what is a short-lived product.

Exam Practice Questions

B1 **1** This question is about alleles.

(a) If the gene for having dimples was dominant, the allele would be written as a D. Which of the following individuals has dimples? Put ticks (✓) in the boxes next to the **two** correct answers. **[1]**

dd ☐   DD ☐   Dd ☐

(b) Complete the genetic cross between a male (with Bb alleles) and a female with bb alleles, using a Punnett square. **[2]**

	♂ Bb	Bb
B	Bb	Bb
b	bb	bb

♀

B1 **2** This question is about genetic disorders.

(a) Which of the following are symptoms of cystic fibrosis?
Put ticks (✓) in the boxes next to the **three** correct answers. **[3]**

Runny nose ☐   Nausea ☐   Ear ache ☐   Breathing difficulties ☑

Thick mucus in lungs ☑   Forgetfulness ☑   Chest infections ☐   Swollen glands ☐

(b)

> Every pregnancy should be tested for Huntington's disease and the fetus aborted if the condition is present.

Linda

> At least people live to middle age before the symptoms of Huntington's disease start to develop.

Jamie

Write a response to Linda explaining why her idea is potentially unethical. **[6]**

🖉 *The quality of written communication will be assessed in your answer to this question.*

B3 **3** What are the two ways that humans have directly caused an organism's extinction? **[2]**

B2 **4** The following statements describe the different stages in the vaccination process. They are in the wrong order. Fill in the empty boxes to put the stages in the correct order. **[2]**

A The markers on the surface of the microorganism trigger the production of specific antibodies by white blood cells.

B The white blood cells capable of fighting the microorganism remain in the bloodstream.

C The modified microorganism is injected into the body.

D A harmful microorganism is modified so that it is incapable of multiplying.

E The microorganism is destroyed before it causes harm.

Start ☐ ☐ ☐ ☐ ☐

B1 **5** Explain the disadvantages of making genetic testing compulsory. **[6]**

✎ *The quality of written communication will be assessed in your answer to this question.*

B2 **6** Label the heart. **[3]**

right atrium — left atrium

right valves — left valves

right ventricle — left ventricle

HT **B1** **7** Draw straight lines to join each term to the **best** available explanation. **[4]**

Term	Explanation
Genotype	A version of a gene
Phenotype	Possessing two of the same alleles
Allele	The characteristics expressed in the environment
Heterozygous	Possessing one of each allele type
Homozygous	The alleles present for a gene in an individual
	A gene

B2 **8** Which of the following is the **best** explanation for why at least 95% of the population needs to be vaccinated? Put a tick (✔) in the box next to the correct answer. **[1]**

This level stops the disease from spreading between vaccinated people. ☐

People with the disease cannot pass it on. ☑

Enough of the population is vaccinated to avoid an epidemic. ☐

95% ensures the maximum profit for the medical company. ☐

B3 **9** A caterpillar takes in 60kJ of energy. It loses 54kJ of energy through movement, other body processes and waste. The caterpillar is then eaten by a blackbird. What percentage of energy entering the caterpillar is transferred to the blackbird? 6 kJ **[2]**

Module C1 (Air Quality)

Air pollutants can affect the environment and our health. However, there are options available for improving air quality in the future. This module looks at:

- the chemicals that make up air and the ones that are pollutants
- data about air pollution
- the chemical reactions that produce air pollutants
- what happens to pollutants in the atmosphere
- the steps that can be taken to improve air quality.

Chemicals in the Air

The Earth is surrounded by a thin layer of gases called the **atmosphere**. Air forms part of the atmosphere. It is a mixture of different gases consisting of small molecules with large spaces between them. Air contains about 78% **nitrogen**, 21% **oxygen**, 1% **argon and other noble gases**. There are also small amounts of **water vapour**, **carbon dioxide** and **particulates**. The amount of water vapour and polluting gases varies as a result of human activity or by natural processes (e.g. volcanoes).

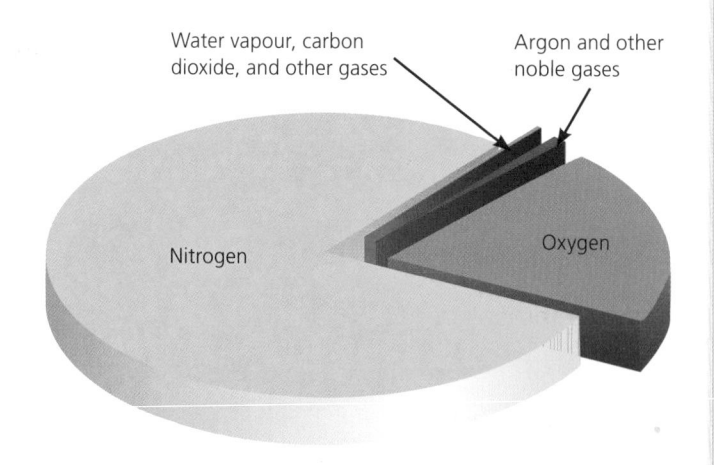

Water vapour, carbon dioxide, and other gases

Argon and other noble gases

Nitrogen

Oxygen

The Earth's Atmosphere

Since the formation of the Earth, 4.6 billion years ago, the atmosphere has changed a lot. The timescale, however, is enormous because one billion years is one thousand million (1 000 000 000) years!

Formation of the Earth

4 billion years ago

3 billion years ago

2 billion years ago

1 billion years ago

Now

The earliest atmosphere contained ammonia, water vapour and carbon dioxide. These gases came from inside the Earth and were often released through the action of volcanoes.

As the temperature of the planet fell, the water vapour in the atmosphere condensed to form the oceans and seas.

The evolution of photosynthesising organisms started to reduce the amount of carbon dioxide and increase the amount of oxygen in the atmosphere.

Carbon from carbon dioxide in the air became locked up in sedimentary rocks as carbonates and fossil fuels after dissolving in the oceans.

Clean air contains about:
- **78% nitrogen**
- **21% oxygen**
- **1% other gases**, including 0.035% carbon dioxide.

Normal air contains varying amounts of **water vapour** and some **polluting gases**. The variation in the quantities of these gases is partly due to human activities.

Pollutants in the Air

Pollutants are chemicals that can harm the environment and our health.

Pollutants that harm the environment can also harm humans indirectly. For example, acid rain makes the water in rivers and lakes too acidic for plants and animals to survive. This has a direct impact on our food chain and natural resources like trees.

Pollutant	Harmful to.	Why?
Carbon dioxide	Environment	Traps heat in the Earth's atmosphere (a greenhouse gas).
Nitrogen oxides	Environment Humans	Cause acid rain. Cause breathing problems and can make asthma worse.
Sulfur dioxide	Environment	Causes acid rain.
Particulates (small particles of solids, e.g. carbon)	Environment Humans	Make buildings dirty. Can make asthma and lung infections worse if inhaled.
Carbon monoxide	Humans	Displaces oxygen in the blood, which can result in death.

Measuring Pollutants

By measuring the **concentrations** of pollutants in the air, it is possible to assess air quality. The units of measurement used are **ppb** (**parts per billion**) or **ppm** (**parts per million**). For example, a sulfur dioxide concentration of 16ppb means that in every one billion (1 000 000 000) **molecules** of air, 16 will be sulfur dioxide molecules.

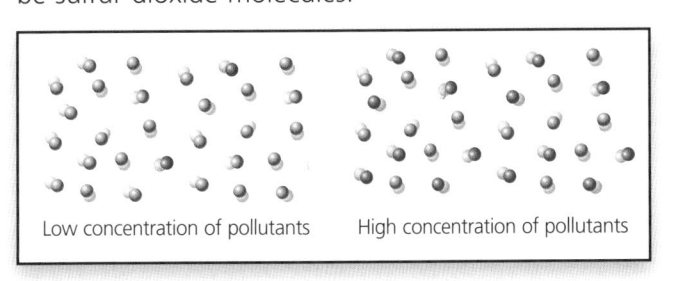
Low concentration of pollutants   High concentration of pollutants

Data about Pollution

Data is very important to scientists because it can be used to test a theory or explanation.

Example

One theory states that carbon monoxide (CO) is an example of a pollutant caused by human activity.

If this is true, carbon monoxide concentrations are likely to be higher in densely populated areas, e.g. cities.

The data below was collected on the same day using a carbon monoxide meter:

Location	Time	Carbon Monoxide Concentration (ppm)
City centre	9.00am	5.2
	10.00am	4.9
	11.00am	5.0
	12.00pm	2.6
	1.00pm	4.8
Country park	9.00am	0.2
	10.00am	0.1
	11.00am	0.1
	12.00pm	0.0
	1.00pm	0.1

Measurements like this can vary because:

- **variables** (factors that change), like the volume of traffic and weather, affect concentrations
- all measuring **equipment** has limited accuracy
- the user's **skill** will affect the accuracy of the measurement.

Because the measurements vary, it is not possible to give a **true value** for the concentration of carbon monoxide in the air. However, the true value is likely to lie somewhere within the **range** of the collected data, i.e. between 4.8 and 5.2 in the city centre and between 0 and 0.2 in the country park. The measurement of 2.6ppm has been excluded from the data range for the city centre because it is an **outlier**. Outliers are measurements that stand out as being very different from the rest of the data. They normally indicate some sort of error.

Data about Pollution (Cont.)

HT You must be able to say why 2.6ppm is an outlier, e.g. the operator may have misread the scale. It is unlikely that the volume of traffic would have decreased at midday. In fact, you might expect it to increase as people leave their workplaces for lunch.

It is important that measurements are repeated. If you look at one measurement on its own, you cannot tell if it is reliable. However, if you look at lots of repeated measurements, any errors should stand out.

By calculating the **mean** (finding the average) of a set of repeated measurements, you can overcome small variations and get a **best estimate** of the true value.

$$\text{Mean} = \frac{\text{Sum of all values}}{\text{Number of values}}$$ Do not use outliers in mean calculations!

$$\text{City} = \frac{5.2 + 4.9 + 5.0 + 4.8}{4} = \textbf{5.0ppm}$$

$$\text{Country} = \frac{0.2 + 0.1 + 0.1 + 0.0 + 0.1}{5} = \textbf{0.1ppm}$$

The mean carbon monoxide concentration in the city centre is significantly higher than the mean carbon monoxide concentration in the country park. So, this data supports the theory that carbon monoxide is a pollutant caused by human activity.

In fact, about half of all carbon monoxide emissions in the UK are produced by road transport, with the rest coming from homes and other industries.

HT There is a **real difference** between the mean carbon monoxide concentrations in the city centre and the park because the difference between the mean values is a lot bigger than the range of each set of data. If the difference between the mean values had been smaller than the range, there would have been no real difference. The result would have been insignificant and the data would not support the theory.

Chemicals

Elements are the 'building blocks' of *all* materials. There are more than 100 elements and each one is made up of very tiny particles called **atoms**. All the atoms of a particular element are the **same** and are unique to that element.

Each element is represented by a different **chemical symbol**, e.g. C for carbon, O for oxygen and Fe for iron.

Atoms can join together to form bigger building blocks, called **molecules**.

Compounds are formed when the atoms of **two or more different elements** are **chemically combined**. The properties of a compound are very different to the properties of the individual elements it is made from.

Chemical symbols and numbers are used to write **formulae**. Formulae show:

- the different elements that make up a compound
- the number of atoms of each different element in one molecule.

Example

A water molecule, H_2O:

$$H_2O$$

Each molecule has…   two hydrogen atoms   one oxygen atom

N.B. You should be able to match the formulae given on the following pages to visual representations of the molecules.

Chemical Change

During a **chemical reaction** new substances are formed from old ones. This is because the atoms in the **reactants** (starting substances) are rearranged in some way:

- Joined atoms may be separated
- Separate atoms may be joined
- Joined atoms may be separated and then joined again in different ways.

These chemical changes are **not** easily reversible. You can show what happens during a chemical reaction by using a word equation. The reactants are on one side of the equation and the **products** (newly formed chemicals) are on the other.

Reactants $\longrightarrow$ Products

Oxidation and Reduction

An example of **oxidation** is a chemical reaction that occurs when oxygen joins with an element or compound. An example of **reduction** is when oxygen is lost from a substance.

Combustion

Combustion is a chemical reaction that occurs when fuels burn, releasing energy as heat. For combustion to take place, **oxygen** must be present. Combustion is an example of oxidation.

Coal is a fossil fuel that consists mainly of carbon. The following equation shows what happens when coal is burned in air:

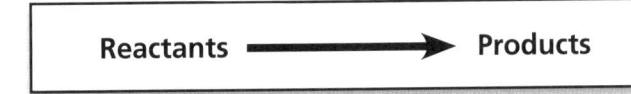

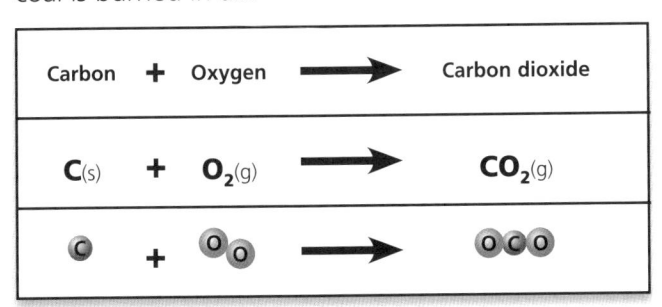

This equation tells us that one atom of carbon (solid) and one molecule of oxygen (gas) produce one molecule of carbon dioxide (gas).

No atoms are lost or produced during a chemical reaction. So, there will **always** be the same number of atoms on each side of the equation, therefore conserving mass. This means there will always be some pollutants formed during the combustion of fuels.

HT The conservation of atoms during combustion reactions has implications for air quality since some atoms in the fuel may react to give products that are pollutants, e.g. carbon monoxide or sulfur dioxide.

Burning Fossil Fuels

Many of the pollutants in the atmosphere are produced through the combustion of fossil fuels, e.g. in power stations, cars, aeroplanes, etc.

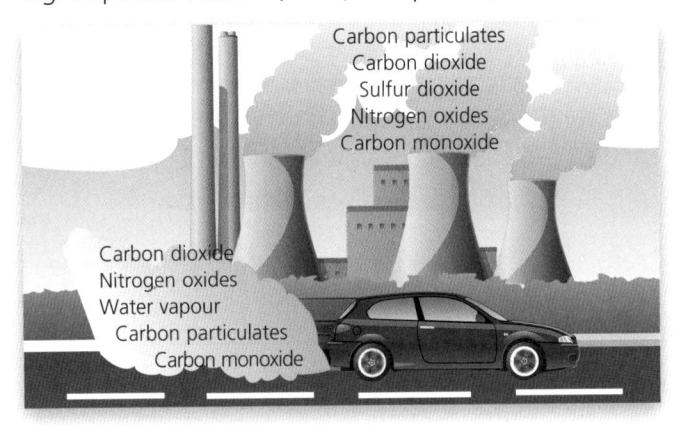

Carbon particulates
Carbon dioxide
Sulfur dioxide
Nitrogen oxides
Carbon monoxide

Carbon dioxide
Nitrogen oxides
Water vapour
Carbon particulates
Carbon monoxide

Complete Combustion

Fossil fuels, such as petrol, diesel fuel, natural gas and fuel oil, consist mainly of compounds called **hydrocarbons**. A hydrocarbon contains *only* **hydrogen** atoms and **carbon** atoms. So, when it is burned in air, **carbon dioxide** and **water** (hydrogen oxide) are produced. This is called **complete combustion**. Remember, carbon dioxide is a pollutant!

If the fuel burns in pure oxygen, the reaction is more rapid than when it burns in air.

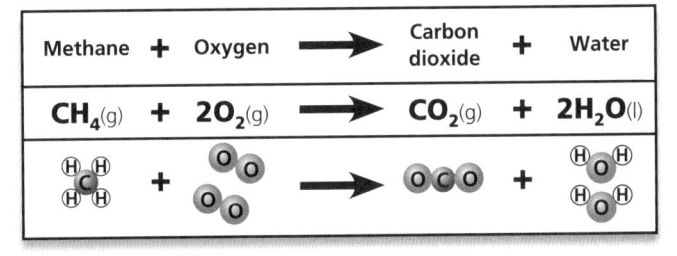

Incomplete Combustion

If a fuel is burned and there is not enough oxygen in the air, **carbon particulates** (**C**) or **carbon monoxide** (**CO**) may be produced. This is called **incomplete combustion**.

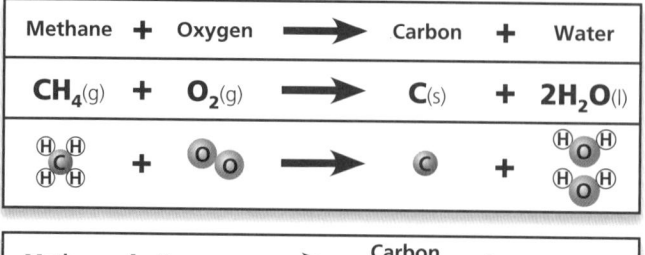

Methane	+	Oxygen	⟶	Carbon	+	Water
$CH_4{}_{(g)}$	+	$O_2{}_{(g)}$	⟶	$C_{(s)}$	+	$2H_2O_{(l)}$

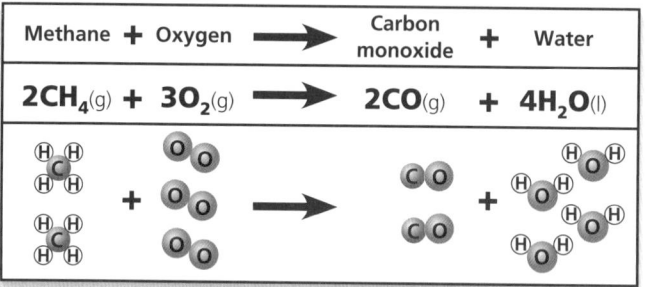

Methane	+	Oxygen	⟶	Carbon monoxide	+	Water
$2CH_4{}_{(g)}$	+	$3O_2{}_{(g)}$	⟶	$2CO_{(g)}$	+	$4H_2O_{(l)}$

Incomplete combustion occurs in car engines, so exhaust emissions contain carbon particulates and carbon monoxide, as well as carbon dioxide.

Many samples of coal contain sulfur, so sulfur dioxide is released into the atmosphere when they are burned.

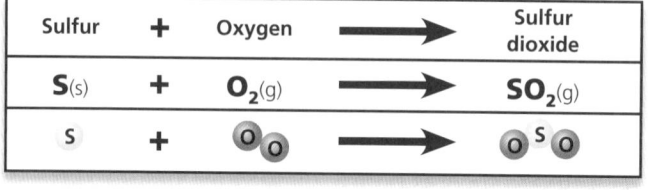

Sulfur	+	Oxygen	⟶	Sulfur dioxide
$S_{(s)}$	+	$O_2{}_{(g)}$	⟶	$SO_2{}_{(g)}$

During the combustion of fuels, high temperatures (e.g. in a car engine or power station) can cause **nitrogen** in the atmosphere to react with **oxygen** and produce **nitrogen oxides**.

HT The nitrogen oxides are formed in two steps:
1 The nitrogen reacts with oxygen to form nitrogen monoxide.

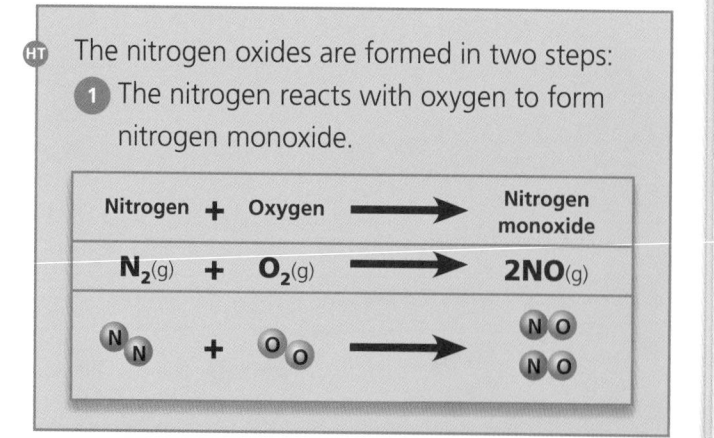

Nitrogen	+	Oxygen	⟶	Nitrogen monoxide
$N_2{}_{(g)}$	+	$O_2{}_{(g)}$	⟶	$2NO_{(g)}$

HT **2** Nitrogen monoxide is then **oxidised** to produce **nitrogen dioxide**.

Nitrogen monoxide	+	Oxygen	⟶	Nitrogen dioxide
$2NO_{(g)}$	+	$O_2{}_{(g)}$	⟶	$2NO_2{}_{(g)}$

When NO and NO_2 occur together they are called oxides of nitrogen and they are written as NO_x.

What Happens to Pollutants?

Once pollutants have been released into the atmosphere, they cannot just disappear; they have to go somewhere. This is when they can start causing **problems** for the environment.

Carbon particulates are **deposited** on surfaces such as stone buildings, making them dirty. The appearance of many beautiful old buildings has been changed owing to this.

Some **carbon dioxide** is removed by natural processes; it is needed by plants for **photosynthesis** and some also **dissolves** in rainwater and seawater, where it reacts with other chemicals in the water.

However, because we are producing **too much** carbon dioxide, not all of it is used up naturally. The rest remains in the atmosphere, so each year the concentration of carbon dioxide in the atmosphere increases.

Because carbon dioxide is a **greenhouse gas** (it traps heat in the atmosphere), the rise in concentration is contributing to **global warming**, which is leading to **climate change**.

Sulfur dioxide and **nitrogen dioxide** dissolve in water to produce **acid rain**. Acid rain can damage trees, erode stonework, corrode metal and upset the pH balance of rivers and lakes. If water is too acidic, plants and animals will die and the whole food chain will be affected.

Identifying Health Hazards

Because humans need to breathe in air to get oxygen, it is reasonable to assume that air quality will have some effect on the body.

To find out exactly how air quality affects us, scientists look for **correlations** (patterns) that might link a **factor** (e.g. a pollutant in the air) to an **outcome** (e.g. a respiratory complaint like asthma).

Example

We now know that **pollen** in the air causes **hay fever** in people who have a pollen **allergy**.

However, to reach this conclusion, scientists had to look at thousands of medical records. The data showed that most cases of hay fever occurred in the summer months when pollen counts were high.

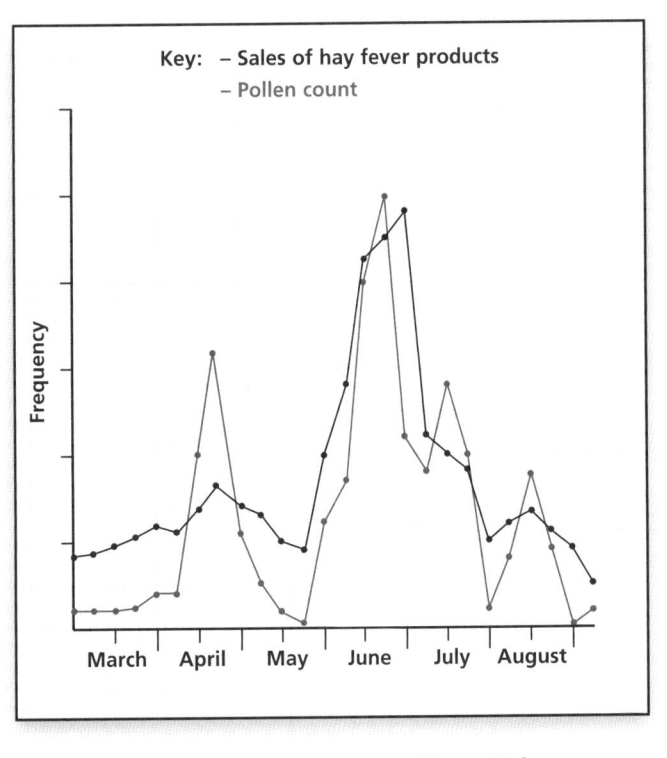

Key: – Sales of hay fever products
– Pollen count

This correlation suggested that pollen **might** cause hay fever. However, it did not provide conclusive evidence because there were lots of other variables that could have influenced the outcome, e.g. temperature, humidity, other pollutants, etc.

Further investigations, in the form of **skin tests**, were carried out to find out how pollen can affect health.

Pollen was collected in spore traps. The pollen was then stuck to the skin of volunteers using plasters.

In some volunteers the skin became red and inflamed, indicating an **allergic reaction**. The results showed that people with a pollen allergy also suffered from hay fever. Those who did not have a pollen allergy did not get hay fever. This provided much stronger evidence of a link between pollen and hay fever.

When these findings were released, other scientists studied the data and repeated the skin test experiments. The fact that the tests always produced the same results proved that they were reliable.

Another condition that is linked to air quality is asthma. However, this example is more complicated. Studies of asthma have shown that when the concentration of NO_2 (nitrogen dioxide) increases in the air, more asthma attacks are triggered.

However, people still have asthma attacks when the levels of nitrogen dioxide are very low. This suggests that although nitrogen dioxide can increase the chance of an asthma attack, it is not the primary **cause**.

There are many factors that can trigger an asthma attack. To fully understand which factors **cause** asthma and which factors may **aggravate** the condition, scientists need to study a large sample of people.

Improving Air Quality

Air pollution affects everyone, so we all have a responsibility to reduce it.

Motor vehicles and power stations that burn fossil fuels are two major sources of atmospheric pollution, so we need to look at how emissions from these sources can be reduced.

Emissions from power stations can be reduced by:

- using less electricity so fewer fossil fuels need to be burned
- removing toxic chemicals before they are burned, e.g. removing the sulfur from natural gas and fuel oil
- using alternative renewable sources of electricity, e.g. solar energy, wind energy and hydroelectric energy, to replace fossil fuels
- using a filter system to remove sulfur dioxide and particulates (carbon and ash) from flue gases before they leave a coal-burning power station's chimney.

> **HT** The sulfur dioxide is removed from flue gases by **wet scrubbing**, using an alkaline slurry or seawater.
>
> During wet scrubbing, the flue gas containing the sulfur dioxide is brought into contact with a slurry of either limestone (calcium carbonate) or lime (calcium oxide) and water. The alkaline slurry is usually sprayed onto the pollutant gas flow, where the sulfur dioxide is absorbed onto its surface. The absorbed sulfur dioxide is then converted to calcium sulfate.
>
> During seawater scrubbing, flue gases are washed with seawater, which dissolves the sulfur oxides. The acidic dissolved sulfur oxides will react with alkalis, such as hydrogencarbonates present in the seawater, to produce sulfate salts.

Emissions from motor vehicles can be reduced by:

- buying a car with a modern engine that is more efficient and burns less fuel
- buying a hybrid car, which uses electric power in the city centre and can then switch to running on petrol for longer journeys
- using a low-sulfur fuel (readily available) to reduce the amount of sulfur dioxide released
- converting the engine to run on biodiesel, which is a renewable fuel
- using public transport to reduce the number of vehicles on the road
- making sure cars are fitted with **catalytic converters**, which reduce the amount of carbon monoxide and nitrogen monoxide emitted.

The reactions that occur in a catalytic converter are:
- Carbon monoxide is oxidised to carbon dioxide by gaining oxygen.

Carbon monoxide	+	Oxygen	$\longrightarrow$	Carbon dioxide
$2CO_{(g)}$	+	$O_{2(g)}$	$\longrightarrow$	$2CO_{2(g)}$

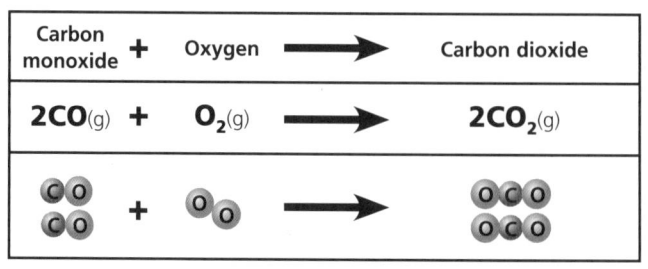

- Nitrogen monoxide is reduced to nitrogen by losing oxygen.

Nitrogen monoxide	+	Carbon monoxide	$\longrightarrow$	Nitrogen	+	Carbon dioxide
$2NO_{(g)}$	+	$2CO_{(g)}$	$\longrightarrow$	$N_{2(g)}$	+	$2CO_{2(g)}$

The only way of reducing carbon dioxide emissions is to burn fewer fossil fuels.

Global Choices

In 1997 there was an international meeting about climate change in **Kyoto**, Japan. People from many nations agreed to reduce carbon dioxide emissions, and targets were set for individual countries. The governments of the countries are required to take appropriate measures to meet the targets.

National Choices

Here are some of the initiatives that are helping the UK meet its target:

- Setting legal limits for vehicle exhaust emissions, which are enforced by statutory mot (ministry of transport) tests
- Making catalytic converters compulsory on new vehicles
- Using subsidies (grants) or reduced taxes to encourage power companies to use 'cleaner' fuels
- Introducing a car tax system that encourages drivers to buy smaller cars with smaller engines
- Encouraging investment in non-polluting renewable energy such as wind and solar energy.

These initiatives will impact on many areas of science and industry. For example, when new cars are developed, the technology used must meet all the legal requirements.

Some governments are concerned that steps taken to reduce carbon dioxide emissions will result in a decline in manufacturing and production, employment and the national economy.

Local Choices

Many local authorities are trying to encourage us to make environmentally friendly choices by providing:

- doorstep collections of paper, bottles, metals and plastics for recycling
- regular bus and train services
- electric trams (in some cities)
- congestion charges
- 'park and ride' schemes
- cycle paths and cycle parks.

Personal Choices

It is clear that the **choices** we make as **individuals** affect the amount of pollution in the air.

Using less energy in the home reduces the demand for energy from power stations, e.g. turning off televisions and not leaving them on standby.

Making sure your car is energy efficient and has a catalytic converter, or choosing an alternative mode of transport (e.g. a bicycle), cuts down on vehicle emissions.

Recycling materials like paper, bottles, metals and plastics helps to conserve natural resources but also saves energy, e.g. it takes about 95% less energy to recycle an aluminium can than to make a new one.

There are other benefits to the 'green' options too. For example, walking and cycling instead of travelling by car help to keep us fit!

HT When making national choices, the benefits and needs must be weighed up against all the problems. This could result in different countries making different decisions. For example, there are benefits and problems when using biofuels and electricity to fuel cars.

Fuel	Benefits	Problems
Biofuels	Renewable source that is carbon zero	• A lot of land is needed to grow biomass • Transportation of biomass to the generator
Electricity	No exhaust fumes and a quiet engine	• Lots of charging stations needed • Length of time to recharge batteries • Battery life • Cost

Module C2 (Material Choices)

We use materials for a variety of different functions every day. Materials are often selected for a job because of the properties that they possess. This module looks at:

- the properties and structure of materials
- how polymers are created
- how the properties of materials can be altered
- the importance of nanotechnology.

Natural and Synthetic Materials

The materials that we use are chemicals, or mixtures of chemicals, and include metals, polymers and ceramics. Some materials can be made or obtained from living things, e.g. cotton (plant), paper (wood), silk (a silk worm) or wool (sheep). Synthetic materials, produced by chemical synthesis, can be made as alternatives to these. The raw materials may be taken from the Earth's crust.

Crude Oil

When extracted, crude oil is a thick, black, sticky liquid. It contains mainly **hydrocarbons**, which are chain molecules containing only hydrogen and carbon atoms.

Different hydrocarbons have different boiling points because their molecular chains are different lengths. The strength of the forces between the hydrocarbon molecules increases as the length of the molecule increases. More energy is needed to break the forces between the molecules in the liquid so that they can move freely as a gas. Therefore, larger molecules have higher boiling points. This means that hydrocarbons can be separated by fractional distillation into different parts or **fractions** (groups of hydrocarbons with similar lengths).

The petrochemical industry refines naturally occurring crude oil to produce fuels, lubricants and raw materials for chemical synthesis. Only a small proportion of crude oil is used in chemical synthesis; most of it is used for fuels.

Properties and Uses of Materials

Examples

Unvulcanised Rubbers	
Properties:	**Uses:**
• Low tensile strength	• Erasers
• Soft	• Rubber bands
• Flexible / elastic	

Vulcanised Rubbers	
Properties:	**Uses:**
• High tensile strength	• Car tyres
• Hard	• Conveyor belts
• Flexible / elastic	• Shock absorbers

Plastic – Polythene	
Properties:	**Uses:**
• Light	• Plastic bags
• Flexible	• Cling wrap
• Easily moulded	• Water pipes

Plastic – Polystyrene	
Properties:	**Uses:**
• Light	• Meat trays
• Insulation properties	• Egg cartons
• Water resistant	• Coffee cups
	• Packaging

Synthetic Fibres – Nylon	
Properties:	**Uses**
• Lightweight	• Clothing
• Tough	• Climbing ropes
• Blocks ultraviolet light	

Synthetic Fibres – Polyester	
Properties:	**Uses:**
• Lightweight	• Clothing
• Waterproof	• Bottles
• Tough	

The properties of the materials used will affect the effectiveness of the end product, so manufacturers always test and assess them carefully beforehand.

Example

A supermarket needs to produce carrier bags. It can use either polythene or biodegradable plastic.

One factor that will determine the supermarket's choice of material is strength, so it carries out the following investigation: a 2cm × 20cm strip of each type of plastic is placed in a clamp. (Each strip used is exactly the same size to ensure a fair test). Weights are then gradually attached to the bottom of each strip to find the total weight it can support before breaking.

The experiment is repeated a number of times to ensure the results are reliable.

Measurement	Maximum Weight (N)	
	Polythene	**Biodegradable Plastic**
1	25.45	19.80
2	25.50	19.75
3	25.40	19.80
4	52.50	19.85
5	25.50	19.90

N.B. 1kg weighs 10N.

When analysing data like this, look to see if any values stand out as being unusual, i.e. they look like **outliers**. In the data collected for polythene the fourth measurement is an outlier.

> **HT** The outlier is likely to have been caused by human error, e.g. the investigator writing down the measurement incorrectly. It is discounted.

The range (or span) of each set of data is from the lowest value to the highest value. The **true value** of the measured quantity is likely to lie within this range. Calculating the mean of a set of data helps to overcome any small variations and

obtain a best estimate for the true value of the measured quantity.

> Mean Maximum Weight for Polythene $= \dfrac{101.85}{4}$
>
> $= \textbf{25.46N}$
>
> Mean Maximum Weight for Biodegradable Plastic $= \dfrac{99.10}{5}$
>
> $= \textbf{19.82N}$

This data shows that polythene can support more weight than the biodegradable plastic before breaking. In terms of strength, this makes polythene the most suitable material from which to make carrier bags.

> **HT** On average, the polythene strips can support a weight of 25.46N before breaking, whereas the biodegradable strips can only support 19.82N. Both sets of data show that the range lies within ±0.06N or ±0.08N. This means that, at worst, the polythene strips may break at 25.40N and, at best, the biodegradable strips at 19.90N. This still leaves a difference of 5.50N (25.40 − 19.90), which in terms of strength makes polythene the most suitable material to make the bag from.

However, there are lots of other considerations the supermarket must take into account before making its final decision.

> **HT** Other considerations the supermarket must take into account include:
> - being certain that the data can be reproduced
> - cost
> - biodegradability
> - whether the bags are waterproof or not.

Polymerisation

Polymerisation is an important chemical process in which small hydrocarbon molecules, called **monomers**, are joined together to make very long molecules called **polymers**:

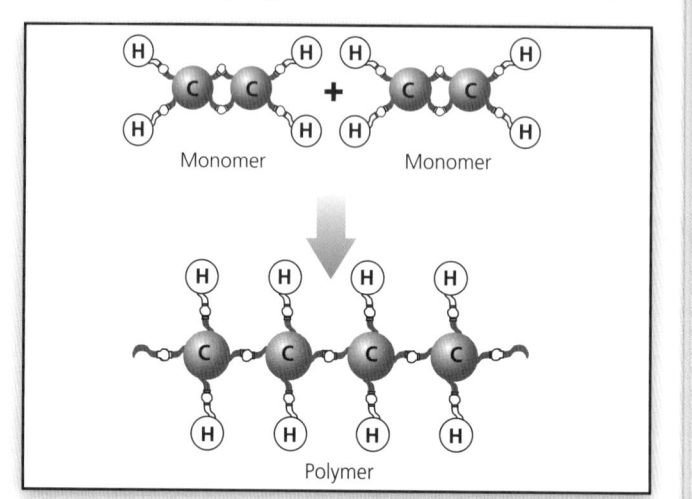

Monomer   Monomer

Polymer

In the example below, the resulting long-chain molecule polymer is polyethene, often called polythene.

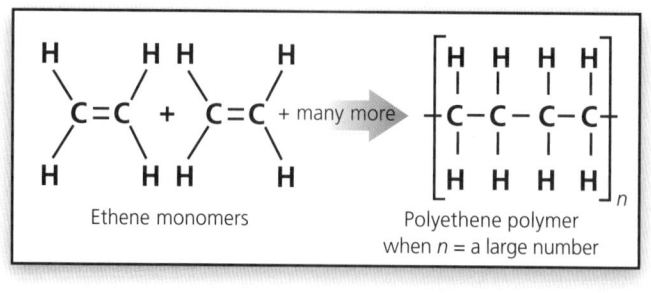

Ethene monomers

Polyethene polymer when n = a large number

Remember that during a chemical reaction the number of atoms of each element in the products must be the same as in the reactants. Count the atoms!

Using Polymerisation

Polymerisation can be used to create a wide range of different materials that have different properties and therefore can be used for different purposes.

Many traditional (natural) materials have been replaced by polymers because of their superior properties.

Polymer	Monomer	Use	Traditional Material	Reason
Polyethene	Ethene	Carrier bags	Paper	Stronger; waterproof
Polychloroethene PVC	Chloroethene	Window frames	Wood	Unreactive; does not rot

Wooden Window Frame   PVC Window Frame

Molecular Structure of Materials

The properties of solid materials depend on how the particles they are made from are arranged and held together.

Natural rubber is very flexible. It consists of a tangled mass of long-chain molecules. Although the atoms in each molecule are held together by strong covalent bonds, there are very weak forces between the molecules so they can easily slide over one another, allowing the material to stretch.

Rubber has a low melting point as little energy is needed to separate the molecules.

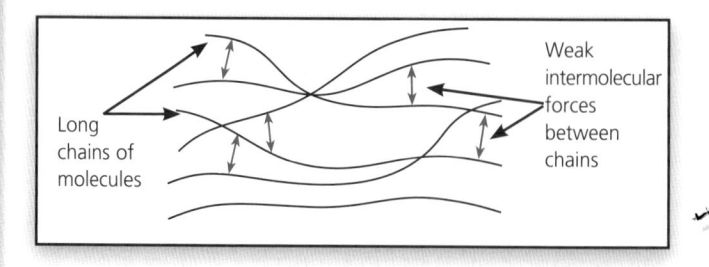

Long chains of molecules

Weak intermolecular forces between chains

Materials with strong forces between the molecules (covalent bonds or cross-linking bridges) have high melting points as lots of energy is needed to separate them.

As the molecules cannot slide over one another, these materials are rigid and cannot be stretched.

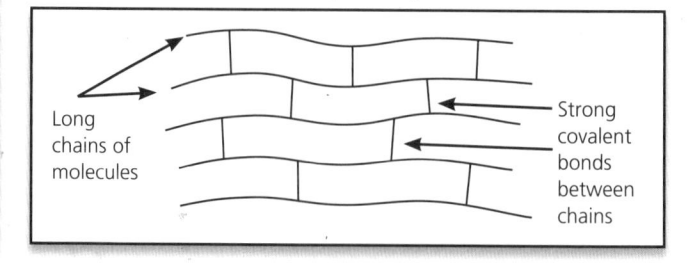

Long chains of molecules

Strong covalent bonds between chains

Modifications in Polymers

Modifications can produce changes to the properties of polymers. These modifications can include:

- **increasing the chain length** – longer molecules are stronger than shorter ones
- **cross-linking** – cross-links are formed by atoms bonding between the polymer molecules, so they are no longer able to move. This makes for a harder material. An example of this is **vulcanisation**, when sulfur atoms form cross-links between rubber molecules. Vulcanised rubber is used to make car tyres and conveyor belts.
- **plasticisers** – adding plasticisers makes a polymer softer and more flexible. A plasticiser is a small molecule that sits between the molecules and forces the chains further apart. The forces between the chains are, therefore, weaker and so the molecules can move more easily. Plasticised PVC is used to make children's toys.

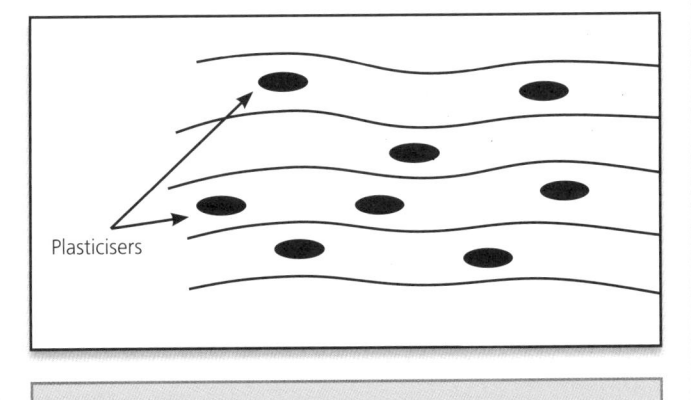

Plasticisers

HT A polymer can also be modified by packing the molecules more closely together to form a **crystalline polymer**. The intermolecular forces are slightly stronger so the polymer is stronger, more dense and has a slightly higher melting point.

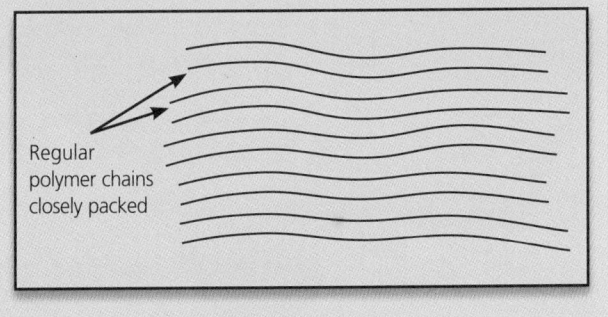

Regular polymer chains closely packed

Nanotechnology

Nanoscience refers to the study of materials that are 1–100 nanometres in size, which is roughly the size of a few atoms. One nanometre is 0.000 000 001m (one billionth of a metre) and is written 1nm or 1×10^{-9}m. (A human hair is around 20 000nm in diameter and a microbe is around 200nm in diameter.)

Nanotechnology is the science of building things on a very tiny scale. It is the understanding and control of matter at dimensions between approximately 1 and 100 nanometres. Nanotechnology is a growing industry.

Nanoscale materials are not new. Naturally occurring materials, such as liposomes and seaspray, have always existed. However, it was not until the early 1980s that they were identified by using scanning tunnelling microscopes.

Nanoscale materials are designed to do specific jobs. For example, nanoparticles of titanium dioxide are added to sunscreen as they are very efficient at absorbing ultraviolet radiation. They are also being developed for use within medicine and dentistry, as well as in the car industry and product-specific catalysts.

Some nanoscale materials are formed accidentally as a result of other chemical reactions, e.g. the smallest particles from the combustion of fuels.

Some Examples of Uses of Nanomaterials

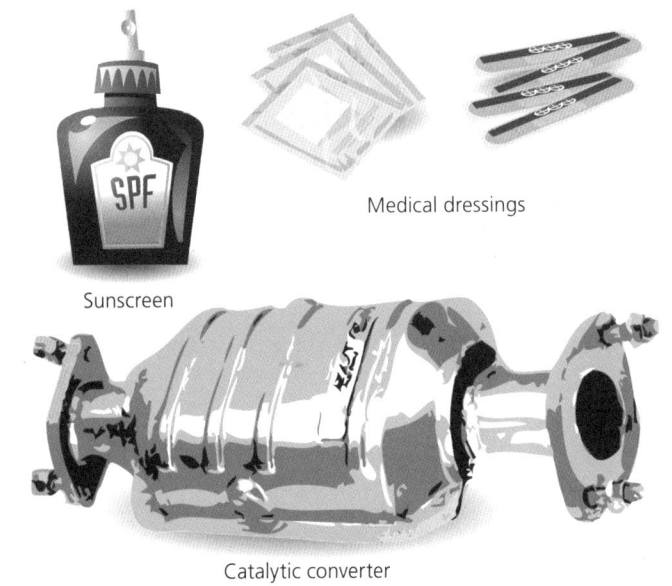

Medical dressings

Sunscreen

Catalytic converter

Properties of Nanoscale Materials

Nanotubes and buckyballs are nanoscale objects made of carbon atoms. They have been used in the manufacture of sports equipment, such as badminton rackets, for many years. In the future they are likely to play an important role in electronic systems.

A Buckyball

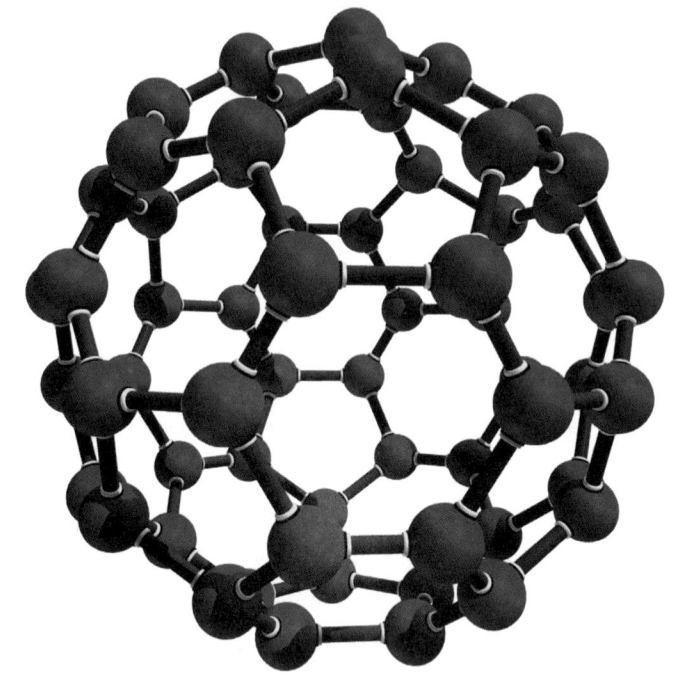

Nanoscale particles have different properties to larger particles of the same material. For example:

- nanoparticle electrons can move through an insulating layer of atoms
- nanoparticles are more sensitive to light, heat and magnetism
- nanoparticles in sunscreens and cosmetics absorb and reflect the harmful ultraviolet rays in sunlight
- nanoparticles can be added to glass to repel water and keep windows clean.

Many of these properties can be explained by the much larger surface area of the nanoparticles compared to their volume.

This means that nanoparticles can be used to modify the properties of existing materials, such as polymers, to make them stronger, stiffer, lighter, etc.

A Magnified Representation of Iron Atoms (Nanoparticles) in a Ring Around Some Surface State Electrons

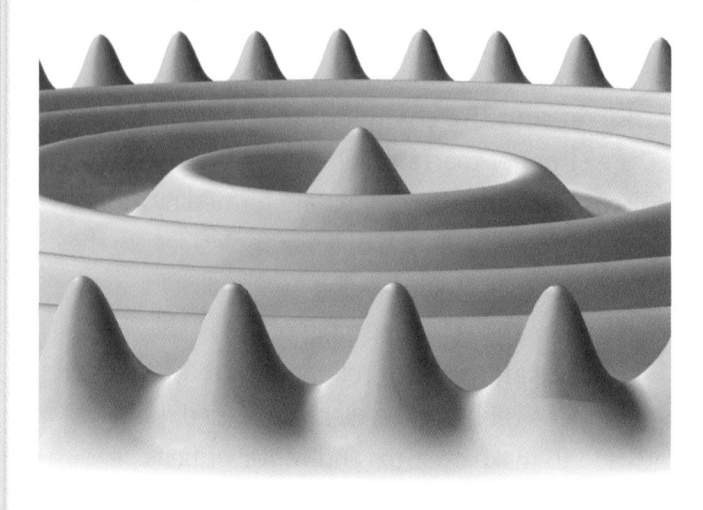

Antibacterial Fibres

In recent years a greater awareness of contact disease transmission and personal hygiene has led to the development of antibacterial fibres to protect wearers against the spread of bacteria and diseases. Researchers have found that silver nanoparticles can destroy many types of bacteria.

Using this knowledge, scientists have developed antibacterial fibres containing silver nanoparticles that are woven into textiles and used to make clothes. Many leading sports-clothing manufacturers now use this silver oxide fibre technology. One of the special features of the clothing is that it has antibacterial properties, which keep the garments fresh.

Nanotechnology in Sports

It is not just the sportswear industry that is using nanotechnology. Nanotechnology is being applied to many sports, e.g. tennis and golf.

Golf clubs are now much lighter, stronger and more efficient than they used to be, thanks to **nanometal** coatings. Nanometals have a crystalline structure and, although they are hundreds of times smaller than traditional metals, they are four times stronger. Golf balls are now treated with nanoscale particles that allow them to travel in straighter lines.

Leading manufacturers of sports equipment have also started adding nanoscale silicon dioxide crystals to tennis rackets. The resulting polymer gives increased performance, without changing the weight.

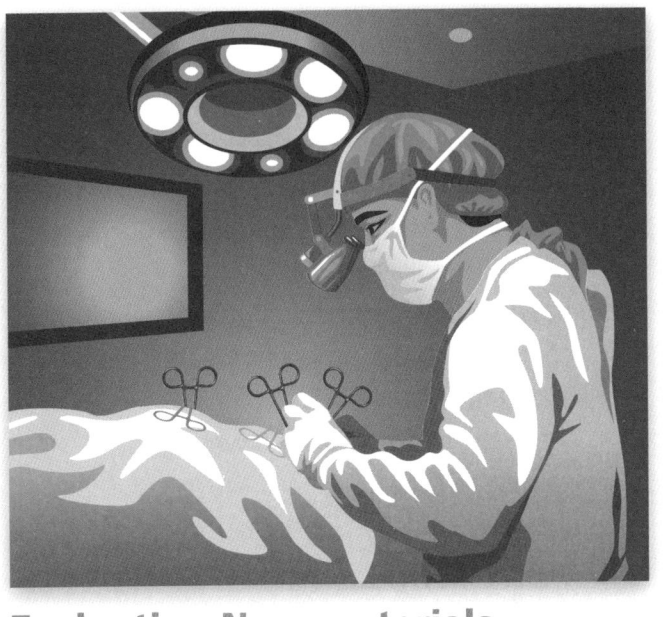

Evaluating Nanomaterials

Nanotechnology is still in the early stages of development. New materials, with very useful properties, are being developed all the time.

Nanotechnology has a variety of potential applications in biomedical, optical and electronic fields. For example, it could be used to create secure communication systems, detect and eradicate small tumours, help in the diagnosis of diseases and help in the development of microscopic surgery that would not leave scars.

It is important to remember that nanoparticles can be dangerous in certain circumstances. For example, nanoparticles in water could be dangerous if they were consumed. Nanoparticles may have other harmful effects on health that are currently not known about.

Some people and organisations are extremely concerned that products with nanoparticles are being introduced before they have been fully tried out and tested. It takes a long time to carry out a full investigation, and any harmful health effects may not be apparent for many years.

Regulations for the development of new techniques and products do exist. A report by the Royal Society suggests that these regulations are adequate to deal with most of the nanotechnology products.

Module C3 (Chemicals in Our Lives: Risks and Benefits)

Britain is a country that has large deposits of valuable minerals, which have been the basis of the chemical industry for more than 200 years. This module looks at:

- the origins of minerals in Britain that contribute to our economic wealth
- plate tectonics
- the importance of salt and where it comes from
- the alkali industry
- making chlorine
- how to make our chemicals safe and sustainable
- life cycle assessment.

The Origins of Mineral Wealth in Britain

Geologists are scientists who study rocks and the processes that formed them. They try to explain the past history of the surface of the Earth by modelling processes that can be observed today.

We know that the Earth's lithosphere (the crust and the upper part of the mantle) is 'cracked' into several large pieces, called **tectonic plates**.

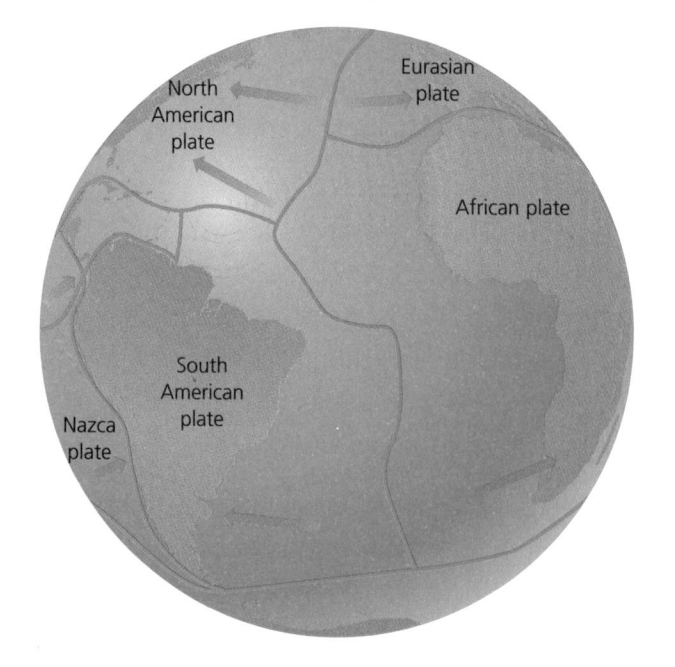

Intense heat, released by radioactive decay deep in the Earth, causes hot molten rock to rise to the surface at the boundary of the plates. This causes the tectonic plates to move very slowly, at speeds of a few centimetres per year.

Geologists use magnetic clues in rocks to track this very slow movement of the plates. They have shown that parts of ancient continents have moved over the surface of the Earth to make up Britain as we know it today. As a result, rocks found in different parts of Britain were formed in different climates.

Over millions of years, a number of processes have led to the formation of valuable resources in Britain, such as coal, limestone and salt. These processes include:

- mountain formation
- erosion
- sedimentation
- dissolving
- evaporation.

These processes form part of the **rock cycle**, which you may have studied during Key Stage 3:

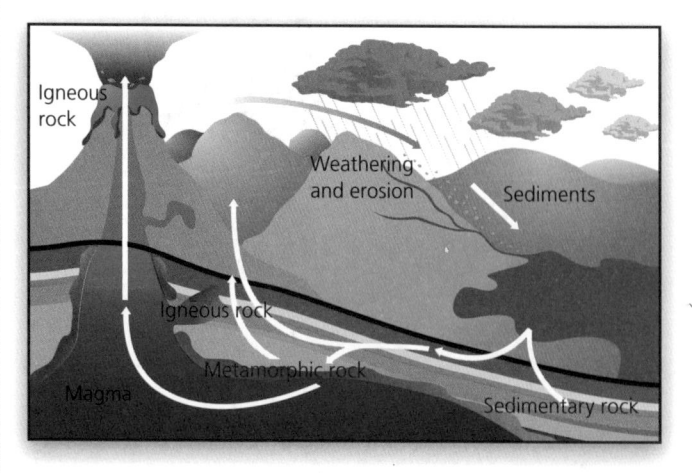

Igneous rocks are formed from molten magma and contain interlocking crystals. Granite and basalt are both igneous rocks.

The formation of sedimentary rocks is described on page 48.

Metamorphic rocks are usually formed from sedimentary rocks subjected to intense heat and pressure. Examples of metamorphic rocks are slate (from shale) and marble (from limestone).

Tectonic Plate Movement

Earthquakes occur at the boundaries of tectonic plates, and mountains are formed when collisions occur between tectonic plates.

1 Plates Slide Past Each Other

When plates slide past each other, huge stresses and strains build up in the crust. These stresses and strains need to be released in order for movement to occur. This 'release' of energy results in an earthquake.

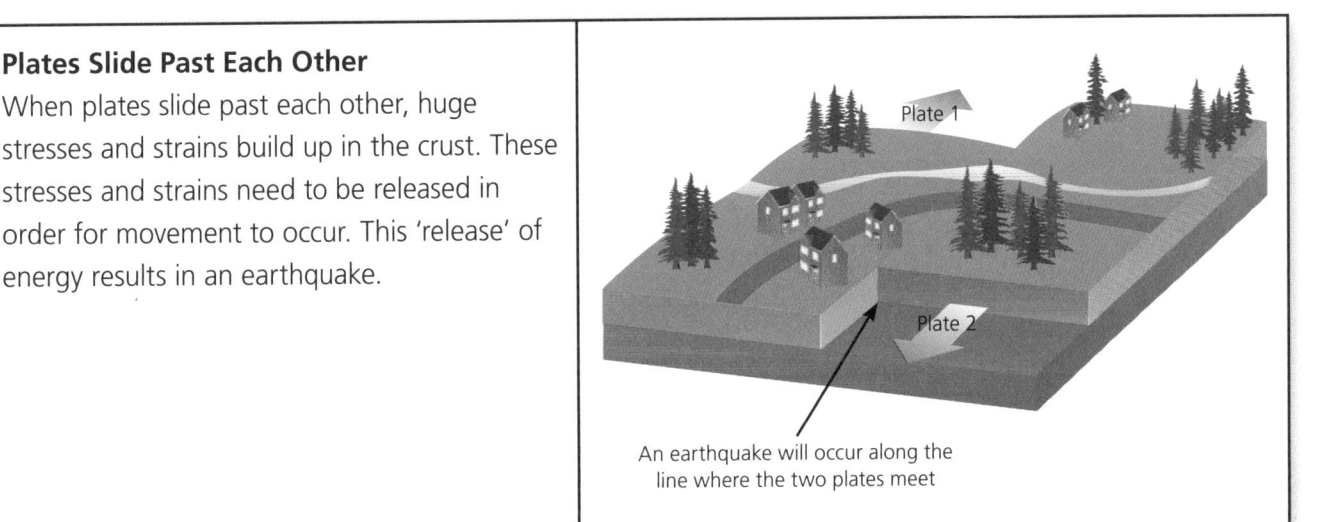

An earthquake will occur along the line where the two plates meet

2 Plates Move Away from Each Other

When plates move away from each other, fractures in the crust occur at the boundary. Molten rock rises to the surface, where it solidifies. Mid-ocean mountain ridges are often formed under the ocean this way.

Islands are made when the new rock builds up above the level of the sea. For example, Iceland is part of the Mid-Atlantic Ridge.

3 Plates Move Towards Each Other

When plates collide, the huge pressures cause the rocks to fold and buckle, resulting in the formation of mountain chains. Sometimes as the plates collide, one is forced under the other and new mountains are made along the plate boundary.

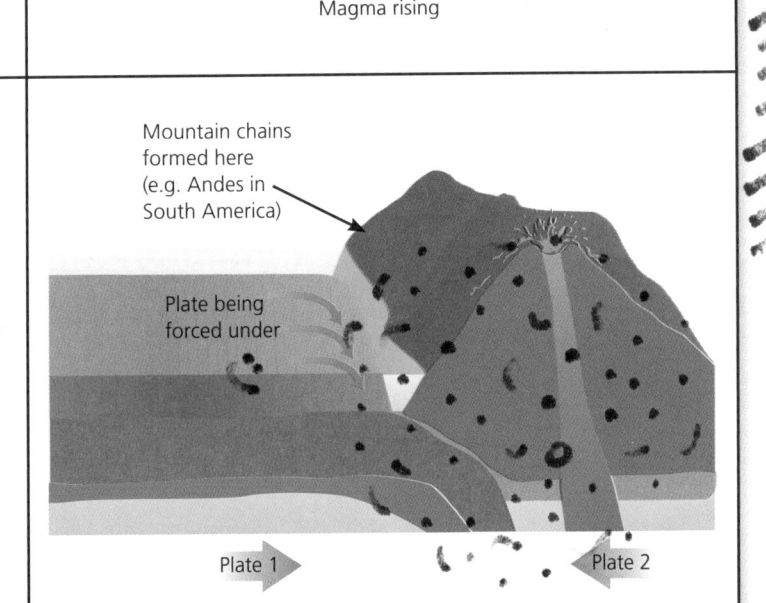

Mountain chains formed here (e.g. Andes in South America)

Plate being forced under

Plate 1   Plate 2

Moving Rocks

As newly formed mountains are exposed to the climate, they are weathered by biological, chemical and physical processes, as shown in the rock cycle. As a result, small fragments of rock are broken off. The fragments are transported, often through rivers, to different places by the process of erosion.

During erosion the fragments are broken down further, into smaller pieces or sediments, as they bump into things. Minerals in the rock, such as salts, dissolve and are carried by the river to different places. Eventually, the river deposits the small sediments on the riverbed or as they enter a lake or the sea. During warm weather water from enclosed lakes **evaporates**, leaving beds of sedimentary **evaporate minerals** including salt crystals.

Organic waste such as leaves, or the skeletons of marine animals, will also be deposited on the river or sea bed. Over millions of years, the layers build up and **sedimentation** occurs. These processes result in the formation of sedimentary rocks such as rock salt, limestone and coal.

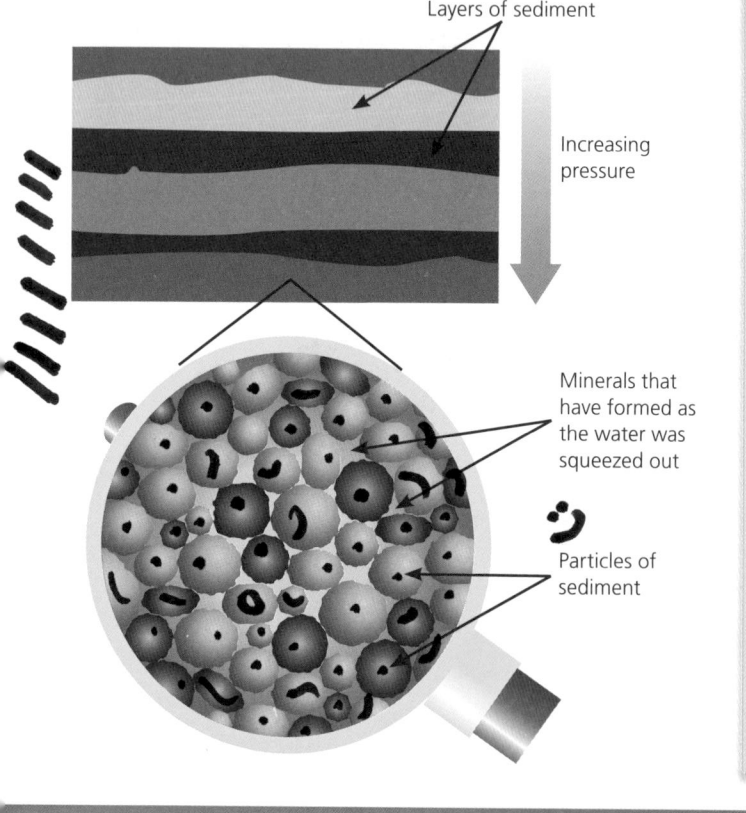

Layers of sediment

Increasing pressure

Minerals that have formed as the water was squeezed out

Particles of sediment

Looking at the Evidence

Today geologists study sedimentary rocks to try to understand how they were formed and where the rocks came from. They look for clues buried in the rocks including:

- fossils
- the presence of shell fragments
- ripples from sea or riverbeds
- the shapes of water-borne grains compared to air-borne grains.

Evidence from Rocks

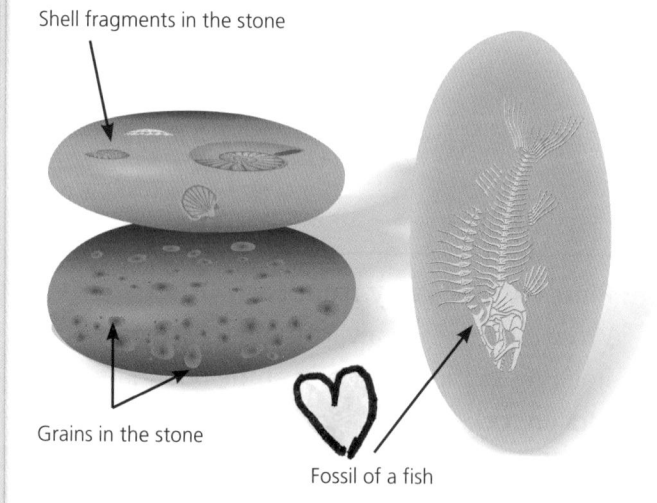

Shell fragments in the stone

Grains in the stone

Fossil of a fish

Exploiting our Natural Resources

The chemical industry developed in the north-west of England because resources such as salt, limestone and coal were available locally. This meant that raw materials could be mined and used in one place, rather than having to be transported to a different part of the country. This made economic sense and provided a good range of jobs for local people.

Salt Mining

Salt can be obtained from the sea or from underground salt deposits. Two different processes are used for extracting the salt from underground deposits. The method used may be determined by how the salt is going to be used.

Method 1: Mining

Rock salt is mined in Cheshire, in the north-west of England. The stages in the process are as follows:

1. Explosives are used to blast the exposed layer of rock salt.
2. The rock salt is loaded into a crusher, where it is ground up into small pieces.
3. A conveyor belt transports the salt to the lift shaft.
4. It is transferred into hoppers and taken to the surface.
5. The salt is then put into large storage areas awaiting collection.

The main use of this rock salt is to treat roads during icy conditions. It is taken by lorry to local authorities throughout the UK.

Under the Cheshire countryside, there are more than 120 miles of empty mine tunnels. The salt mines have also left scars on the landscape, especially where large areas of the ground have been dug out.

Method 2: Solution in Water

Salt is soluble in water. Important industrial chemicals such as chlorine and sodium hydroxide are extracted from salt by the electrolysis of brine (salt solution). Salt can be extracted from the ground in solution and piped directly to the electrolysis plant.

The stages in the process are as follows:

1. Holes are drilled into the salt deposits.
2. Explosive or hydraulics may be used to make the holes larger and so make it easier for the water to penetrate the rock salt.
3. Water is pumped into the bores and the salt dissolves.
4. The salt solution is then pumped back to the surface and piped to the processing plant.

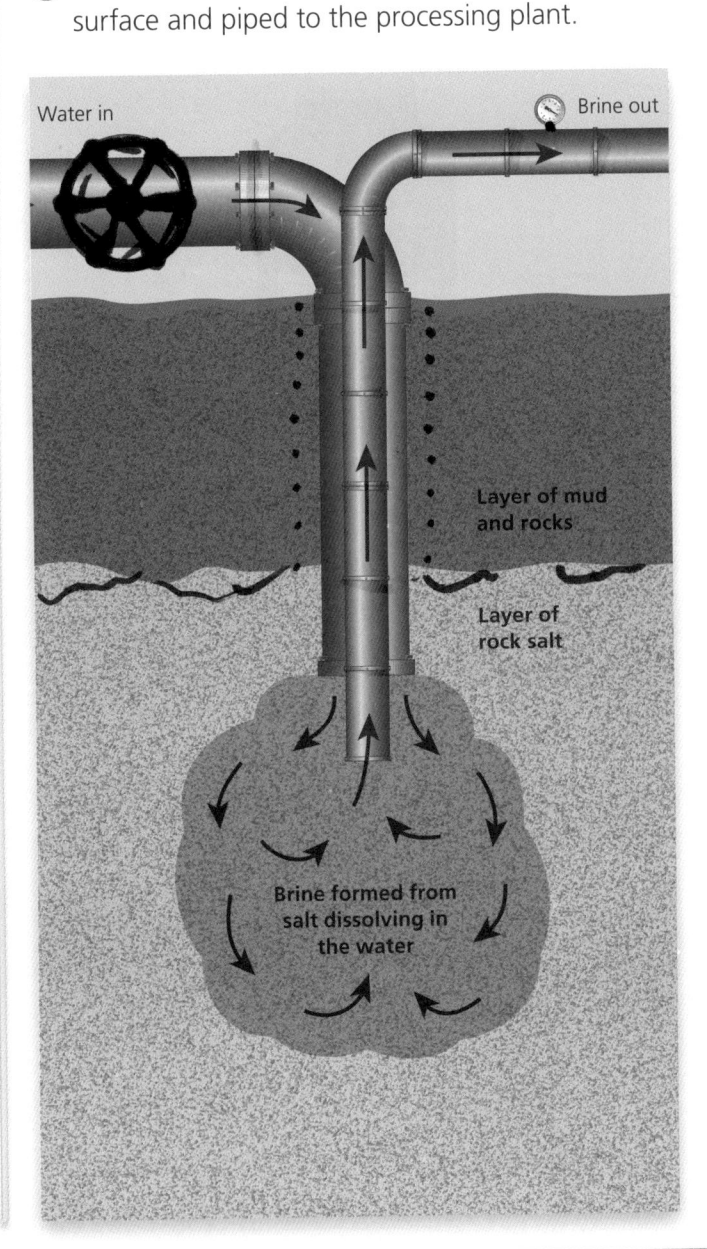

Water in — Brine out

Layer of mud and rocks

Layer of rock salt

Brine formed from salt dissolving in the water

Chemicals in Our Lives: Risks and Benefits

Uses of Salt

Salt (sodium chloride) is a very useful chemical. Here are some of its uses:

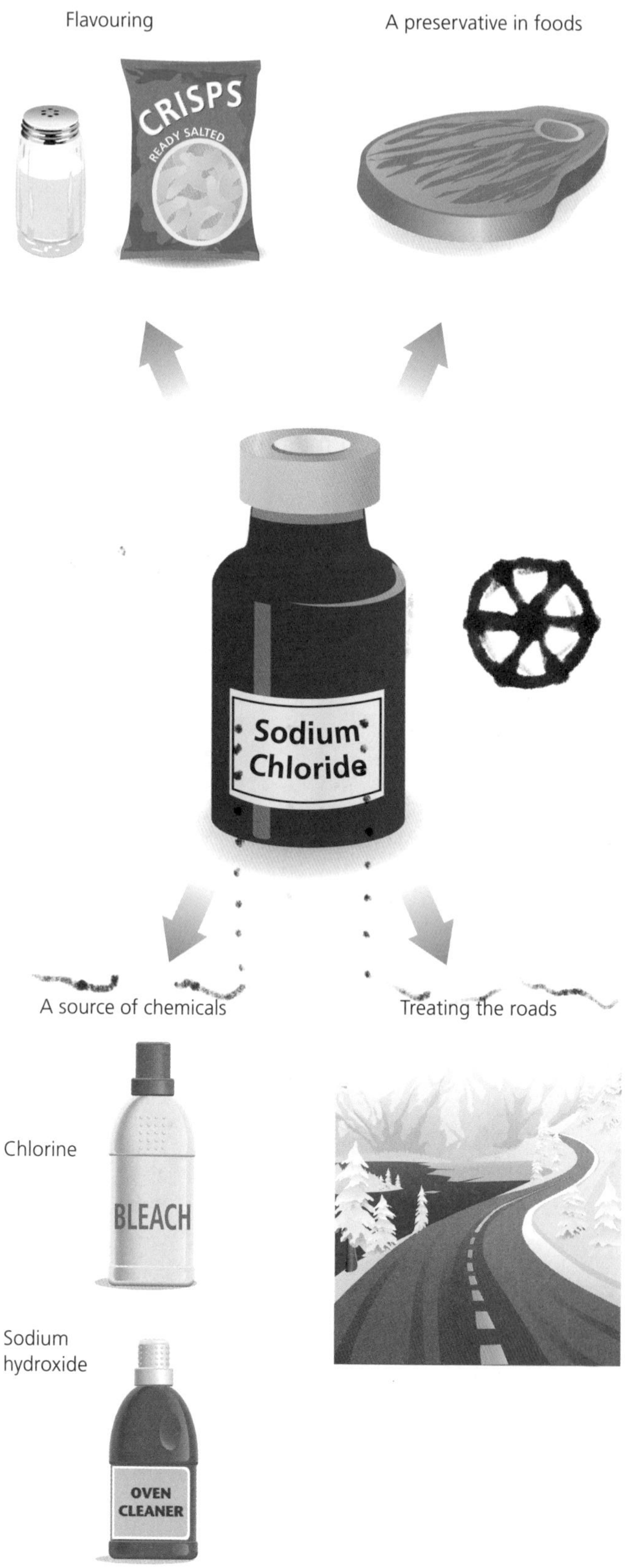

Flavouring

A preservative in foods

Sodium Chloride

A source of chemicals

Treating the roads

Chlorine

BLEACH

Sodium hydroxide

OVEN CLEANER

Salt as a Food Additive

Salt is added to food for flavouring and as a preservative. Sodium is present in additives such as monosodium glutamate and sodium bicarbonate. Processed foods, such as meat and bread products, can be high in salt. Processed foods are thought to account for about 75% of the average person's salt intake.

Salt and Health

Salt is an important component of a healthy diet. It is needed to maintain the concentration of body fluids. It helps cells to take up nutrients and plays a crucial role in the transmission of electrical impulses in the nerves.

However, too much salt is not good for you. When the levels of sodium are too high, it causes water to be retained in the body, which means the volume of fluids increases. Some scientists think that this results in high blood pressure, which can increase the risk of heart attacks and strokes.

Government guidelines recommend that adults should eat 6g of salt a day. However, the average intake of salt is between 9g and 10g a day.

Experts estimate that if average consumption was cut to 6g a day, it would prevent 70 000 heart attacks and strokes a year.

Food and the Government

Government departments, such as the Department of Health and the Department for Environment, Food and Rural Affairs, have a role in making sure that our food is safe, healthy and fairly marketed. They also make sure that food producers are acting within the law. The government departments promote healthy eating and aim to minimise illnesses such as food poisoning. They make sure that food labels are clear and that they say exactly what is in the food.

The food labels help people to decide whether or not to buy the product. For example, coeliacs look for labels that say 'gluten free' and vegetarians look to see if the food contains any animal products. (Some foods also state 'suitable for vegetarians'.)

It is important to give the public the most up-to-date information about food safety. In fact, the Food Standards Agency (FSA), an independent government department, was set up to protect public health and consumer interests in relation to food. Government scientists carry out research into food issues such as **genetically modified** (GM) foods.

Sometimes the research findings are controversial and the results are uncertain. Scientists may even disagree about what the results actually mean. Further problems may be encountered from manufacturers who may not want to accept the research findings, as it may not be in their economic interest.

If there is any doubt about food safety, then one of the scientific advisory committees is asked to carry out a risk assessment. It must decide:

- if the food contains any chemicals that could cause harm
- how harmful the chemicals are
- how much of the food must be eaten before it is likely to harm people
- if any groups of people are particularly vulnerable, e.g. the elderly, children, or those suffering from illness.

HT The outcome of a risk assessment is often based on experience gained from people or animals eating the food.

Sometimes the scientific evidence is uncertain and the risk is unknown, in which case the **precautionary principle** is applied. Both experts and the public are consulted before the regulators make a decision about food safety.

Regulators have to weigh up the costs and benefits of any decision, as the priority is to protect public safety and not just let the new foods be mass produced and put on the market.

For example, many people ask questions such as 'Are GM foods safe to eat?'

For many GM foods, scientists simply do not know enough about the science of altering genes, which may lead to health problems in the future. There is also not much data yet on the potential risks to humans, and this is why the precautionary principle is sometimes applied.

The Alkali Industry

Long before industrialisation, alkalis were used in everyday life. Alkalis are very important chemicals as they neutralise acids to make salts. Traditional sources of alkali included burnt wood and stale urine.

Here are some of the uses of alkalis:
- neutralising acidic soil
- producing chemicals that bind natural dyes to cloth
- producing soap
- producing glass.

HT Alkali compounds are soluble hydroxides and carbonates. They always react with acids in a similar way:

Acid **+** Hydroxide ⟶ Salt **+** Water

Acid **+** Carbonate ⟶ Salt **+** Water **+** Carbon dioxide

Examples

Hydrochloric acid **+** Potassium hydroxide ⟶ Potassium chloride **+** Water

$$HCl_{(aq)} + KOH_{(aq)} \rightarrow KCl_{(aq)} + H_2O_{(l)}$$

Sulfuric acid **+** Potassium hydroxide ⟶ Potassium sulfate **+** Water

$$H_2SO_{4(aq)} + 2KOH_{(aq)} \rightarrow K_2SO_{4(aq)} + 2H_2O_{(l)}$$

Hydrochloric acid **+** Calcium carbonate ⟶ Calcium chloride **+** Water **+** Carbon dioxide

$$2HCl_{(aq)} + CaCO_{3(s)} \rightarrow CaCl_{2(aq)} + H_2O_{(l)} + CO_{2(g)}$$

Nitric acid **+** Calcium carbonate ⟶ Calcium nitrate **+** Water **+** Carbon dioxide

$$2HNO_{3(aq)} + CaCO_{3(s)} \rightarrow Ca(NO_3)_{2(aq)} + H_2O_{(l)} + CO_{2(g)}$$

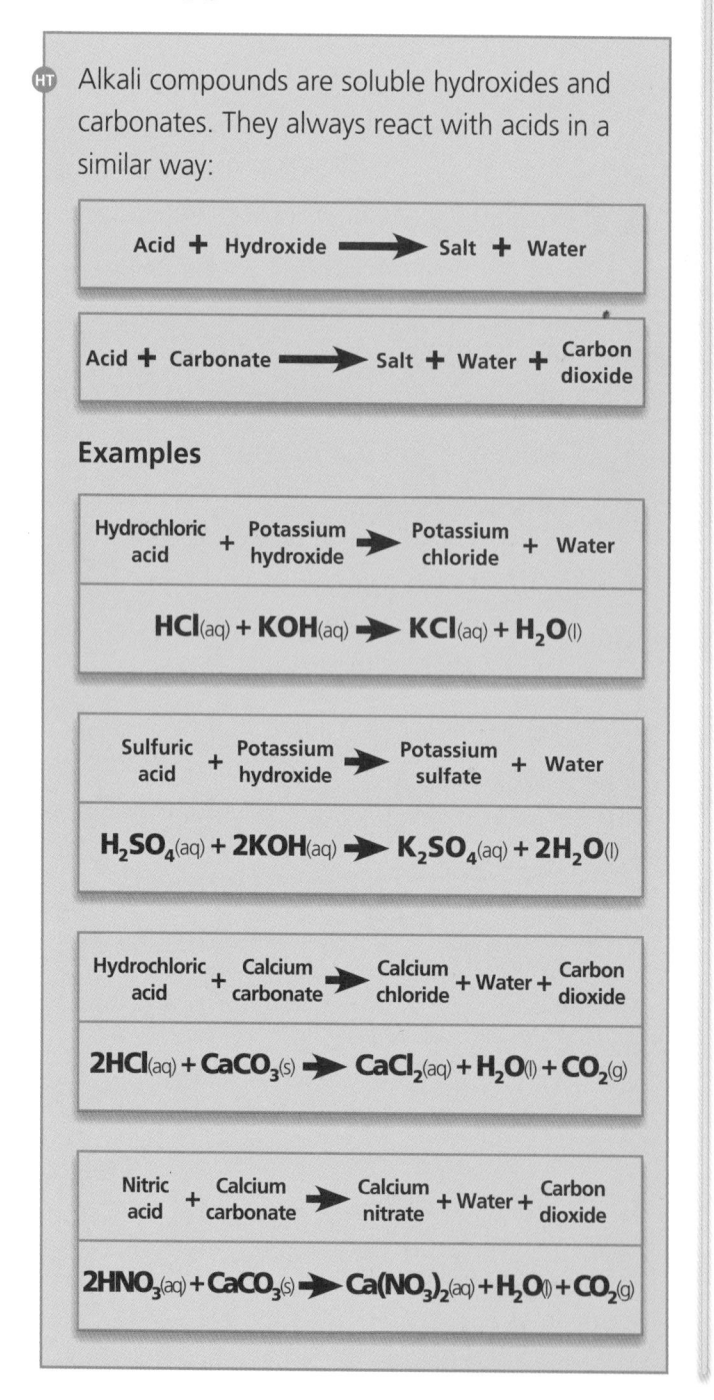

With increased industrialisation, and more demand for alkaline-based products, there was a shortage of alkali in the 19th century. As a result, people looked for other ways of processing alkali.

Early processes for manufacturing alkali from salt and limestone caused a lot of pollution. Large volumes of the acidic gas hydrogen chloride were released into the atmosphere and great heaps of waste that slowly released the toxic and foul-smelling gas, hydrogen sulfide, were also formed.

Industrialists have a responsibility to try to minimise the pollution caused by chemical processes. Sometimes the problems can be solved by converting the waste pollutant into a useful chemical. For example, in this case, by dissolving hydrogen chloride gas in water you can make hydrochloric acid:

Hydrogen chloride **+** Water ⟶ Hydrochloric acid

Alternatively, the hydrogen chloride gas could be used to make chlorine gas by oxidising it.

Hydrogen chloride ⟶ Chlorine **+** Hydrogen

Remember that the properties of compounds are different from those of the elements from which they are made. For example, in the reaction above:
- hydrogen chloride is a colourless, acidic gas
- chlorine is a green gas
- hydrogen is a colourless gas.

Making Chlorine

Chlorine is produced by the electrolysis of brine (sodium chloride solution):

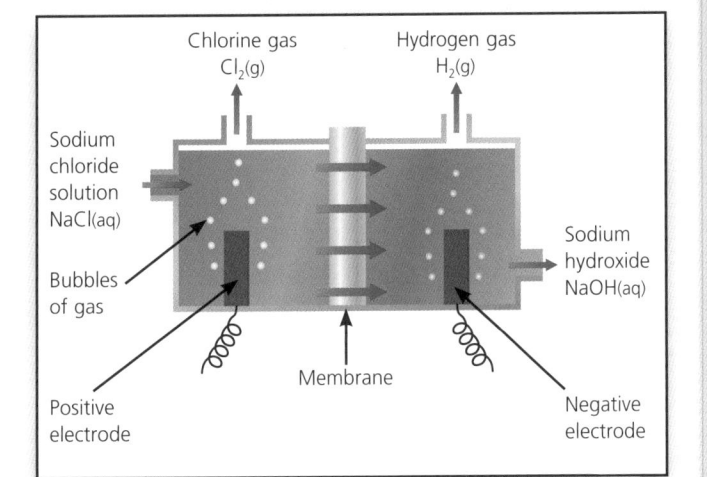

Passing an electric current through the brine causes a chemical change to take place. This forms new products – **chlorine**, **sodium hydroxide** and **hydrogen**. The products have many applications:

- Chlorine is used to kill bacteria in drinking water and swimming pools, and to manufacture hydrochloric acid, disinfectants, bleach and the plastic PVC.
- Sodium hydroxide is used in the manufacture of soap, paper and ceramics.
- Hydrogen is used in the manufacture of ammonia and margarine.

The electrolysis of brine can have an impact on the environment. A major concern is the amount of energy required to carry out electrolysis. A cheap supply of renewable energy is needed.

Water Purification Using Chlorine

Chlorine is added to domestic water supplies to kill any harmful microorganisms that might be present.

Chlorinated drinking water protects against illnesses including:

- typhoid fever
- dysentery
- cholera
- gastroenteritis.

However, chlorinated drinking water will not kill viruses or parasites.

Chlorine was first introduced into drinking water in England in the 1890s and in the USA in 1908.

The graph below shows that, following the introduction of chlorination, there was a decline in the death rate due to typhoid fever in the USA. As more cities across the USA adopted the practice, further reductions were seen until the illness was eliminated in the mid-1940s.

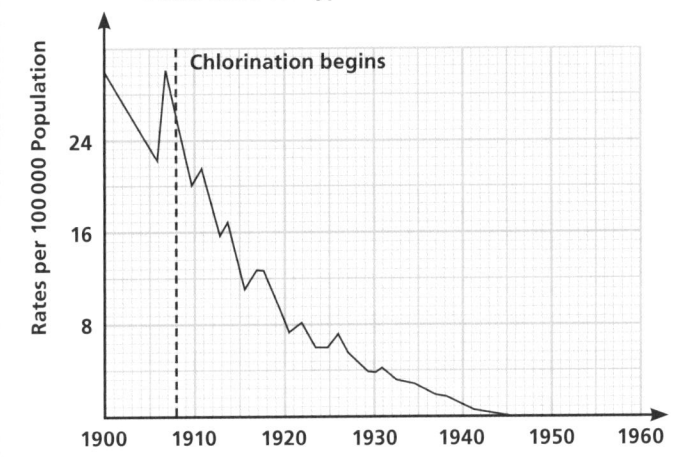

N.B. *You must be able to interpret and make sense of any data connected with the effects of water quality that you are presented with.*

The purification of drinking water by filtration and chlorination is one of the most significant advancements in public health in recent times.

Following natural disasters such as flooding, earthquakes or tsunamis, a lack of clean water becomes the biggest threat to the survivors. This is because people are forced to drink untreated water, which still contains bacteria from deadly diseases.

However, it is possible that there could be other health problems associated with chlorinated water. For example, if there are traces of some organic chemicals in the water (from large and small industrial enterprises, agriculture, transport, etc.), they could combine with chlorine to make chemicals that are harmful to humans.

Water Purification Using Chlorine (Cont.)

Research scientists are continuously investigating these possibilities and offering their advice. From time to time there will be some problems with water quality, such as the scare in North Wales described below.

Water Scare Over

There has been an outbreak of cryptosporidium, a stomach illness that can be caught by drinking infected water. In Anglesey and Gwynedd, there have been 231 reported cases of people catching the bug. As a result, everyone in the North Wales area had to boil their water before consuming it to remove the risk of getting infected.

The infected water is likely to have come from the Llyn Cwellyn reservoir, but health officials have now given North Wales' residents the all-clear; there is no need to continue boiling their water.

However, what remains to be seen is the impact of this scare. General consensus is that people are still wary of their water, and some say they have switched to drinking only bottled water.

Safe and Sustainable Chemicals

Today the pace of scientific and technological development is very fast. New chemicals and materials are being produced continuously. Many materials have useful consumer applications (e.g. in nanotechnology), or they are used in the food industry (e.g. genetically modified foods) or pharmaceutical industry (e.g. for the production of new medicines).

For many new products, scientists have not yet been able to collect enough data to judge whether they are likely to present a risk to the environment and/or human health. Therefore, government departments or individual professionals (e.g. doctors) must decide if the potential benefits outweigh the potential risks.

Given below are some examples where materials were manufactured in large quantities without a potential risk being known.

Thalidomide

In the 1950s, a drug called thalidomide was prescribed to pregnant women to relieve the symptoms of morning sickness. It had been tested on animals and was considered safe to use.

Thousands of babies were subsequently born across the world with serious limb defects and a common factor was found – all the mothers had taken thalidomide in early pregnancy. The drug was withdrawn in 1961. During the initial investigations the drug was never tested on pregnant animals.

Chlorofluorocarbons (CFCs)

In the 1970s, a link was made between CFCs and the destruction of the ozone layer. CFCs had been used in refrigerants and aerosol sprays. Scientists had thought that CFCs were very unreactive molecules, posing no environmental risks.

However, it was discovered that once CFCs are released into the environment, they are carried very large distances into the upper atmosphere where they react with ozone and destroy it.

Potentially, the molecules could be in the environment for 300 years before they react with the ozone.

Polyvinyl Chloride (PVC)

PVC is a polymer that contains carbon, hydrogen and chlorine atoms:

Chloroethene monomers → PVC polymer

Plasticisers can be added to the PVC to make it softer and more flexible, so that the range of uses can be expanded. Scientists have now found that the plasticisers can be leached from the plastic into the surroundings, where they may have harmful effects.

Life Cycle Assessment (LCA)

The life cycle of a product has four phases – **Making the material from natural raw materials**, **Manufacture**, **Use** and **Disposal**. The LCA involves examining each of these phases in detail, including the impact on the environment.

Each part of the life cycle of a product is carefully considered and assessed on the amount of energy and materials (including water) that will be used and how materials will be obtained and disposed of. The outcome of the LCA is dependent on several factors, including the use of the end product.

LCAs were introduced in the 1960s to encourage companies to reduce waste and be aware of environmental impact. New laws were put in place to protect the environment; cash incentives were offered to encourage recycling; and in 1996 a tax was introduced to discourage the use of landfill sites.

The purpose of an LCA is to ensure the most **sustainable** method is used, which means meeting the needs of today's society, whilst allowing for the needs of future generations.

The flow diagram below shows what is being assessed in each stage of an LCA.

Making the material from natural raw materials: Natural raw materials, water and energy needed to make the starting material. Environmental impact from obtaining the natural raw materials.

Manufacture: Resources (including water) and energy needed to make the product. Environmental impact of making the product from the material.

Use: Energy needed to use the product, e.g. fuel and electricity. Energy and chemicals (including water) needed to maintain the product. Environmental impact of using the product.

Disposal: Energy needed to dispose of the product. Environmental impact of landfill, incineration and recycling.

Materials and Their Functions

Different materials can often be used to perform the same job. For example, disposable nappies are made from cellulose fibres, a super-absorbent polymer and fluff pulp, whilst re-usable nappies are made from cloth. Disposable nappies may be more convenient but in a life cycle assessment which one is better for the environment?

The results of one study are shown below.

Impact Per Baby, Per Year	Re-usable Nappies	Disposable Nappies
Energy needed to produce product	2532MJ	8900MJ
Waste water	12.4m^3	28m^3
Raw materials used	29kg	569kg
Domestic solid waste produced	4kg	361kg

The evidence here shows that using re-usable nappies consumes less energy, water and natural resources, whilst also producing less waste. This would suggest that people should be encouraged to use re-usable nappies.

Since 2003 it has been government policy to encourage parents to reduce the number of disposable nappies they use.

The same material can be used to perform different jobs. For example, Teflon® (polytetrafluoroethene), which was accidentally discovered in 1938 by Roy Plunkett, can be used in:
- gaskets and valves
- insulation
- non-stick saucepans
- dentures.

Teflon® is **chemically inert** and temperature resistant, and there is also little impact on the environment when it is disposed of in landfill sites.

Exam Practice Questions

C1 **1** **(a)** The Earth was formed 4.6 billion years ago. The planet's atmosphere at that time was very different to today's atmosphere. Explain how it changed by filling in the empty boxes with the letters to put the stages in the correct order. The first one has been done for you. **[3]**

     A   Water vapour condensed to form oceans.

     B   Volcanic activity released carbon dioxide.

     C   Nitrogen was made as gases reacted with oxygen.

     D   Green plants evolved.

     E   Carbon dioxide levels decreased as oxygen was formed.

B				

(b) Which pie chart represents the current composition of gases in the Earth's atmosphere? Put a tick (✓) in the box next to the correct answer. **[1]**

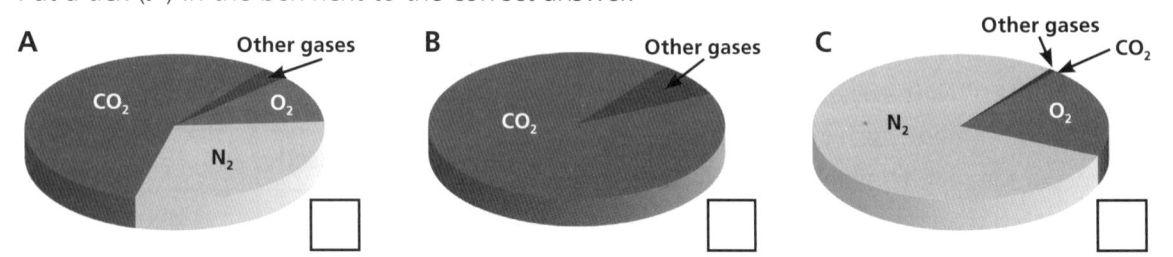

(c) Levels of carbon dioxide in the atmosphere are changing today. Explain how human activity is contributing to these changes. **[6]**

🖉 *The quality of written communication will be assessed in your answer to this question.*

C3 **2** Chlorine was first added to drinking water in England in the 1890s. Shortly after, the USA decided to do the same. The graph shows how the death rates from typhoid fever changed in the USA over a period of 60 years.

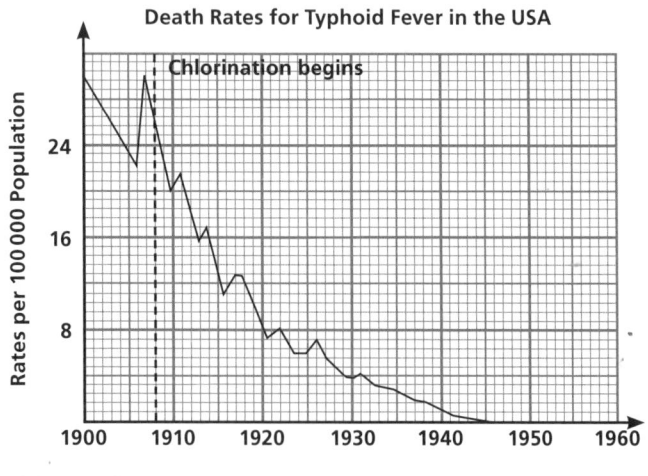

(a) In which year was chlorine first introduced into USA domestic water supplies? **[1]**

(b) Describe what happened to death rates for typhoid fever in the USA over the next 40 years. **[2]**

(c) How did the introduction of chlorine in water supplies produce these results? **[1]**

(d) Does the graph provide sufficient evidence to claim that there is a correlation between chlorinated water and typhoid fever? Explain your answer. **[4]**

C3 **3** Brine (sodium chloride solution) is an important industrial chemical. Passing an electric current through brine causes a chemical change to take place.

Which **three** products come from brine? Put ticks (✓) in the boxes next to the correct answers. **[3]**

Hydrogen gas ☐   Solid sodium chloride ☑   Chlorine gas ☑

Sodium hydroxide ☑   Hydrochloric acid ☐   Oxygen gas ☐

HT **C2** **4** A supermarket needs to produce some new carrier bags. It needs to decide whether to use traditional polythene, a biodegradable material or a UV-degradable material. It decides to carry out a strength test and then find out what the public think. Here are the results:

Test Number	Maximum Weight (N)		
	Polythene	Biodegradable	UV-degradable
1	26.50	19.99	23.48
2	26.53	20.03	23.45
3	26.49	20.01	23.49
4	26.70	19.99	23.46

(a) The supermarket manager takes a quick look at the results and then decides not to do any follow-up work on the biodegradable results. Why do you think he made this decision? **[1]**

(b) How could the manager best estimate the true value of the strength of each bag? **[2]**

(c) The results for the polythene tests contain an outlier. Identify the outlier. **[1]**

(d) Calculate a best estimate of the strength of the polythene bags. **[2]**

(e) Calculate a best estimate of the strength of the UV-degradable bags. **[2]**

(f) The manager asked the public what they thought of the different bags. Here are some of the responses:

The UV-degradable bag is best because it is stronger and better for the environment.

The polythene bag is best because it is stronger and can be re-used and then recycled.

The polythene bag should not be used because it will end up in landfill.

Even though the biodegradable bag is not as strong as the polythene bag, it will decompose over time.

Using the information from the public and the results of the tests, what do you think the manager should do? **[6]**

✏ *The quality of written communication will be assessed in your answer to this question.*

Module P1 (The Earth in the Universe)

Scientific discoveries in the solar system affect our understanding of the planet we live on and our place in the Universe. This module looks at:

- what is known about Earth
- how the Earth's continents have moved and the consequences
- what is known about stars and galaxies
- how scientists develop explanations about Earth and space
- how waves travel.

The Solar System

The **solar system** was formed over a very long period of time, about **5000 million years** ago.

1. The solar system started as **clouds of dust and gas**, which were pulled together by the **force of gravity** (see diagram below).
2. This created intense heat. Eventually, **nuclear fusion** began to take place and a star was born: **the Sun**.
3. The remaining dust and gas formed **smaller masses**, which were attracted to the Sun.

The smaller masses in our solar system are:

- **planets** – eight large masses that orbit (move around) the Sun
- **moons** – small masses that orbit the planets
- **asteroids** – small, rocky masses that orbit the Sun
- **comets** – small, icy masses that orbit the Sun
- **dwarf planets** – small spherical objects that have not cleared their orbits of other objects.

Planets, moons and asteroids all move in **elliptical** (slightly squashed circular) orbits. Comets move in highly elliptical orbits (see diagram below). It takes our planet, Earth, **one year** to make a complete orbit around the Sun.

The Sun

The Sun's **energy** (heat and light) comes from **nuclear fusion**. **Hydrogen** nuclei **fuse** (join) together to produce a nucleus with a larger mass, i.e. a new chemical element. During fusion, some of the energy trapped inside the hydrogen nuclei is released. All the **chemical elements** with a larger mass than helium were formed by nuclear fusion in **earlier stars**.

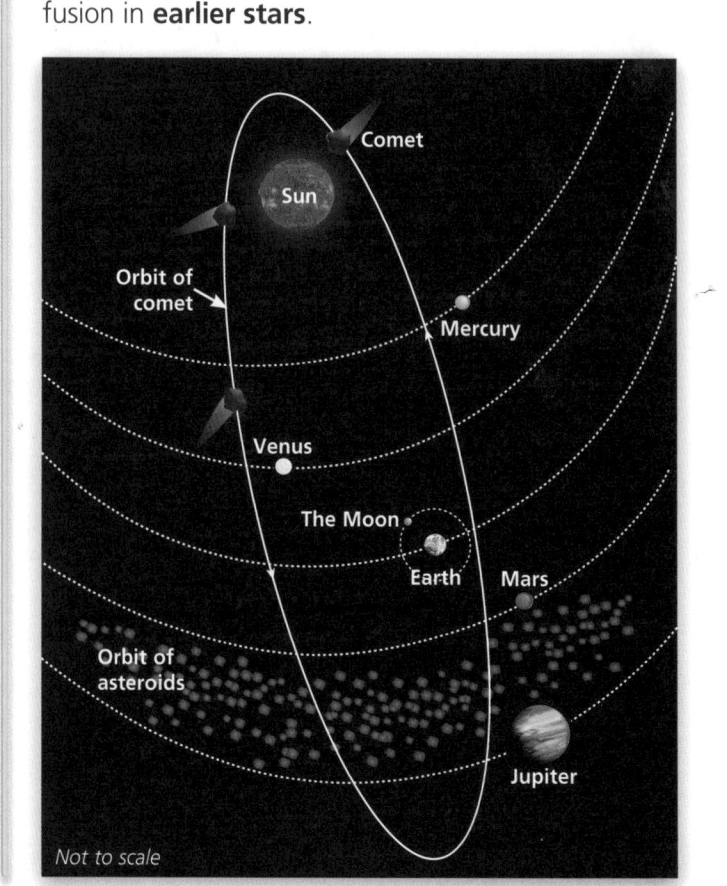

Not to scale

The Universe

At 5000 million years old, the Sun is only 500 million years older than the **Earth**. The **Universe** is much older than this: approximately **14 000 million years old** (almost three times older than the Sun).

The Sun is one of thousands of millions of stars in the Milky Way.

Not to scale

Our galaxy – the Milky Way, 100 000 light-years across, containing at least 100 billion stars

Our galaxy

The Universe – contains billions of galaxies, with vast distances between them

Not to scale

Our planet – the Earth, 12 800km diameter

Our star – the Sun, 100 times wider than Earth

Our Sun

The solar system is approximately 10 billion km across

The Speed of Light

Light travels at very **high but finite** (limited) **speeds**. This means that if the distance to an object is great enough, the time taken for light to get there can be **measured**.

The speed of light is **300 000km/s** in a vacuum (around one million times faster than sound). So, light from Earth takes just over one second to reach the Moon (approximately 384 400km away).

Light from the Sun takes eight minutes to reach the Earth. This means that when we look at the Sun, we are actually seeing what it looked like eight minutes ago.

Vast distances in space are measured in **light-years**. One light-year is the **distance light travels in one year** (approximately 9500 billion km). The nearest galaxy to the Milky Way is 2.2 million light-years away. This means that light from this galaxy has taken 2.2 million years to reach the Earth, and so we are seeing the galaxy as it was in the past.

Measuring Distances in Space

Astronomers work out the distances to different **stars** using two different methods:

1 Relative brightness

In general, the dimmer a star is, the further away it is. However, stars can vary in brightness so we can never be 100% certain.

2 Parallax

If you hold out a finger at arm's length and close each eye in turn, the finger appears to move. The closer the finger is to your face, the more it appears to move. Parallax uses this idea to work out distances.

As the Earth orbits the Sun, stars in the near distance appear to move against the background of very distant stars. The closer they are, the more they appear to move.

The position of a star is measured at six-monthly intervals. These measurements can then be used to calculate its distance from Earth. However, the further away the star is, the more difficult and less accurate the measurement is.

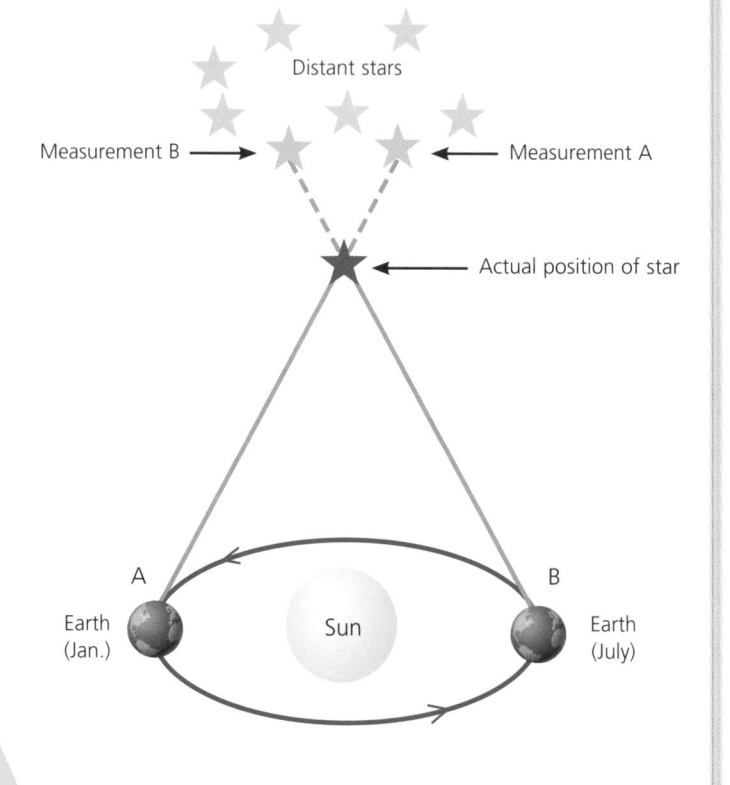

Distant Stars

Because the stars are so far away, everything we know about them is worked out from the **radiation** they produce: **visible light** and other types of radiation, including **ultraviolet** and **infrared**.

All our electric lights on Earth illuminate the night sky, so it is very difficult to see the stars sometimes. This is called **light pollution**. In 1990 the **Hubble Space Telescope** was launched. It orbits the Earth at a height of 600km, so it is not affected by light pollution or atmospheric conditions.

Other Galaxies

If a source of light is moving away from us, the **wavelengths** of the light are **longer** than they would be if the source was stationary.

The wavelengths of light from almost all **galaxies** are longer than scientists would expect. This means the **galaxies are moving away from us**.

HT In 1929 Edwin Hubble discovered that light from distant galaxies had even longer wavelengths. Therefore, they must be moving away from us faster. As a result, he developed **Hubble's Law**:

The speed at which galaxies are moving away from us is proportional to their distance from us (i.e. the faster a galaxy is moving, the further away it is).

If all the galaxies are moving away from one another, this must mean that space is **expanding** (getting bigger).

Redshift

If a wave source is moving away from or towards an observer, there will be a change in the observed wavelength and frequency.

If a source of light moves away from an observer, the wavelengths of the light in its spectrum are longer than if it was not moving. This is known as **redshift** because the wavelengths 'shift' towards the red end of the spectrum.

All distant galaxies appear to be 'redshifted', which means they are moving away from us.

The Beginning

When scientists trace the paths of galaxies, they all appear to be moving away from the same point.

There have been many theories about how the Universe began. The one that best explains this evidence is the **Big Bang** theory, which says that the Universe started with a **huge explosion 14 000 million years ago**.

The End

It is difficult to predict the fate of the Universe because it is very hard to measure the very large distances involved. It is also very difficult to study the motion of very distant objects.

The future depends on the amount of **mass** in the Universe. If there is not enough mass, the Universe will keep expanding. If there is too much mass, gravity will be strong enough to pull everything back together and the Universe will collapse with a big crunch. Measuring the amount of mass in the Universe is very difficult, so its ultimate fate is hard to predict.

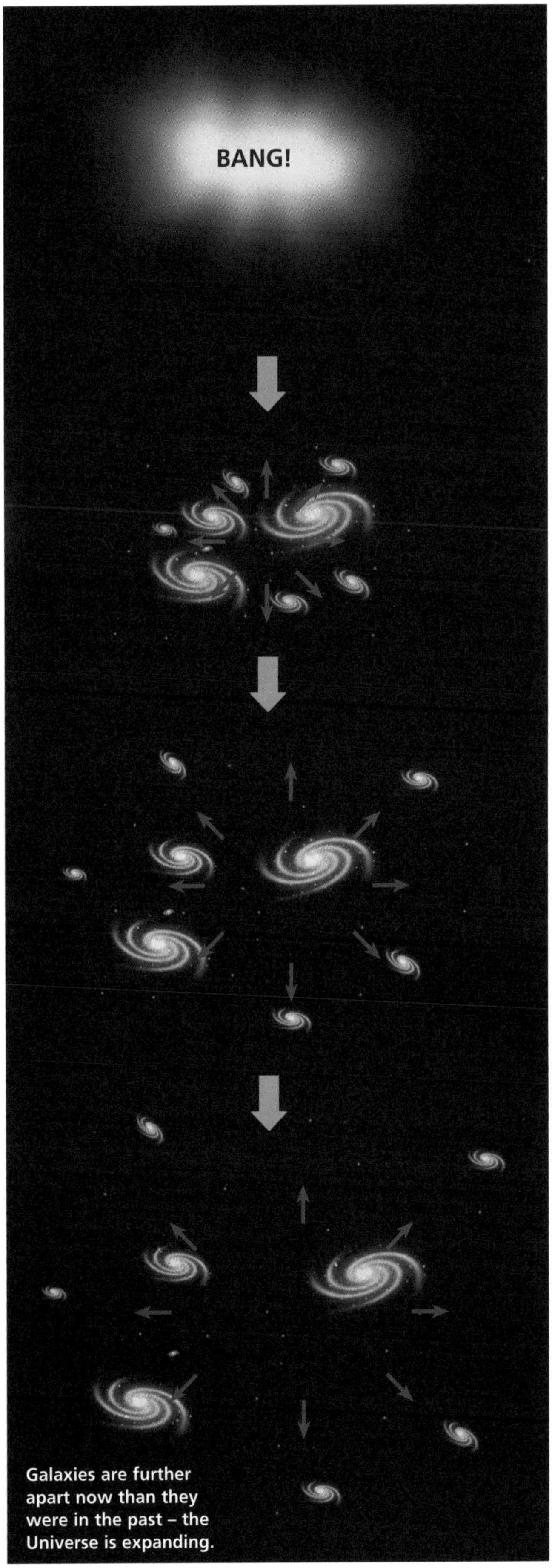

BANG!

Galaxies are further apart now than they were in the past – the Universe is expanding.

The Earth

People once thought that the Earth was only 6000 years old. There was no way of testing this theory, so people believed it for a long time.

We now know that **rocks** provide evidence of how the Earth has changed and clues as to its age.

Erosion – the Earth's surface is made up of **layers** of rock, one on top of the other, with the oldest at the bottom. The layers are made of compacted **sediment**, which is produced by weathering and **erosion**. Erosion changes the surface of the planet over long periods of time.

Craters – the surface of the Moon is covered with impact **craters** from collisions with meteors. However, the Earth, which is much larger, has had fewer meteor collisions (due to Earth's atmosphere), but craters have also been erased by erosion.

Mountain formation – if new **mountains** were not being formed, the whole Earth would have been worn down to sea level by erosion.

Fossils – plants and animals trapped in layers of sedimentary rock have formed **fossils**, providing evidence of how life on Earth has changed over millions of years.

Folding – some rocks look as if they have been **folded** like plasticine. This would require a big force to be applied over a long period of time – further evidence that the Earth is very old.

Radioactive dating – all rocks are **radioactive**, but the amount of radiation they emit **decreases** over time. Radioactive dating measures radiation levels to find out how old they are.

Scientists estimate that the Earth is around **4500 million years old** – it has to be older than its oldest rocks – and when it was first formed it was completely **molten** (hot liquid) and would have taken a very long time to cool down.

The oldest rocks that have been found on Earth are about **4000 million years old**.

The Structure of the Earth

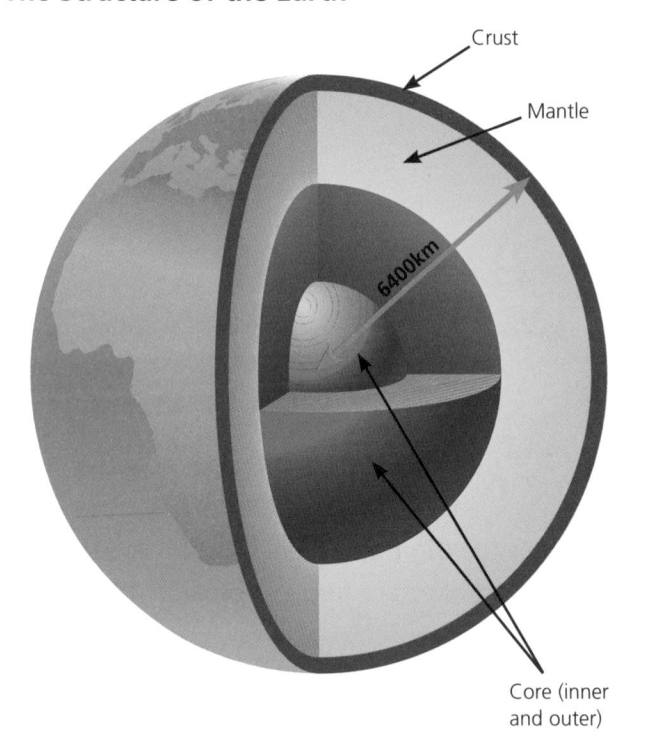

Crust

Mantle

6400km

Core (inner and outer)

Thin rocky crust:
*   Its thickness varies between 10km and 100km.
*   Oceanic crust lies beneath the oceans.
*   Continental crust forms continents.

The mantle:
*   Extends almost halfway to the centre.
*   Has a higher density, and a different composition, than rock in the crust.
*   Very hot, but under pressure.

The core:
*   Made of nickel and iron.
*   Over half of the Earth's radius; has a liquid outer part and a solid inner part.
*   The decay of radioactive elements inside the Earth releases energy, which keeps the interior of the Earth hot.

Continental Drift

Alfred Wegener (1880–1930) was a meteorologist who put forward a theory called **continental drift**.

He saw that the continents all fitted together like a jigsaw, with the mountain ranges and sedimentary rock patterns matching up almost perfectly. There were also fossils of the same land animals on different continents. Wegener proposed that the different continents were once joined together, but had become separated and drifted apart.

How It Once Was

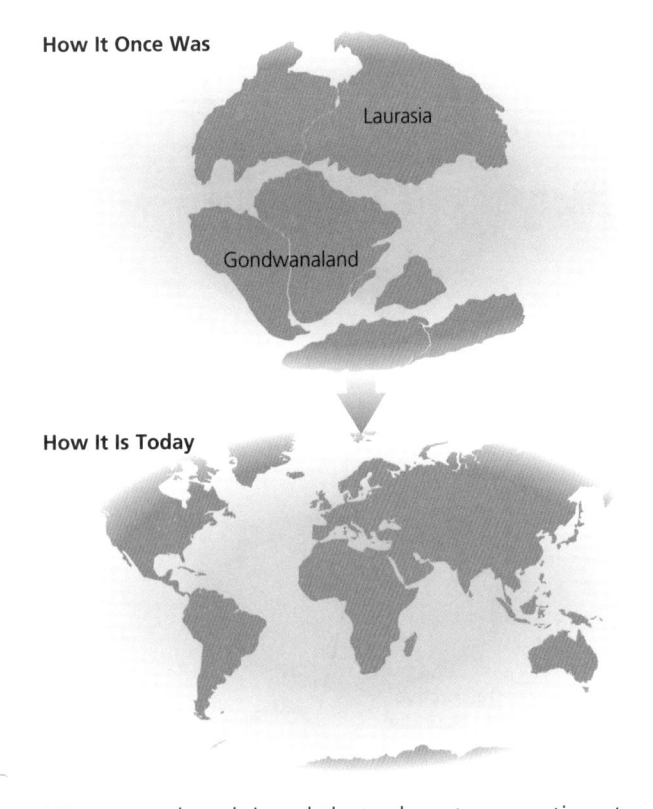

How It Is Today

Wegener also claimed that when two continents collided, they forced each other upwards to make mountains.

Geologists at the time did not accept Wegener's theory because:

- he was not a geologist and was therefore considered to be an outsider
- it was a big idea but he was not able to provide much evidence
- the evidence could be explained more simply by a land bridge connecting the continents that has now sunk or been eroded
- the movement of the continents was not detectable.

Wegener's evidence for continental drift could be summarised as:

- similar patterns of rocks, which contain fossils of the same plants and animals, e.g. the Mesosaurus
- closely matching coastlines.

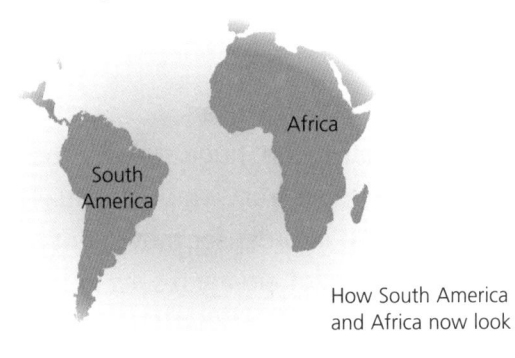

How South America and Africa now look

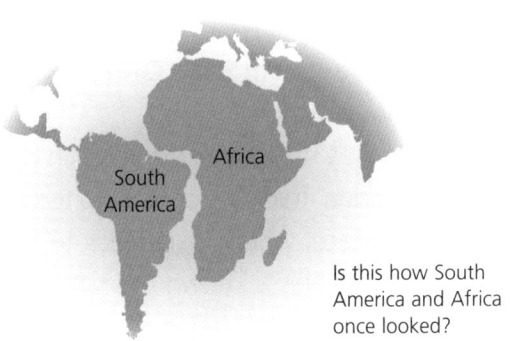

Is this how South America and Africa once looked?

Tectonic Plates

We now know that the Earth's crust is cracked into several large pieces called **tectonic plates.**

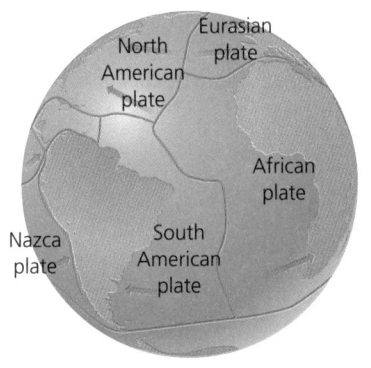

The plates float on the Earth's mantle because they are less dense. They can move apart, move towards each other or slide past each other. The lines where the plates meet are called **plate boundaries**. These are where **volcanoes**, **earthquakes** and **mountain building** normally occur.

Earthquakes that occur near coastlines or at sea can often result in a **tsunami** (similar to a tidal wave).

Tectonic Plate Movement

The movement of the tectonic plates can happen suddenly due to a build up in pressure and can sometimes have disastrous consequences, e.g. earthquakes and tsunamis. Tectonic plates can move in three ways:

1 Slide Past Each Other

When plates slide, huge stresses and strains build up in the crust which eventually have to be released in order for movement to occur. This 'release' of energy results in an earthquake. A classic example of this is the West Coast of North America (especially California).

2 Move Away from Each Other – Constructive Plate Boundaries

When plates move away from each other at an oceanic ridge, fractures occur. Molten rock rises to the surface, where it solidifies to form new ocean floor. This is known as seafloor spreading. Because new rock is being formed, these are called **constructive** plate boundaries.

3 Move Towards Each Other – Destructive Plate Boundaries

As plates are moving away from each other in some places, it follows that they must be moving towards each other in other places. When plates collide, one is forced under the other, so these are called **destructive** plate boundaries. Earthquakes and volcanoes are common on destructive plate boundaries.

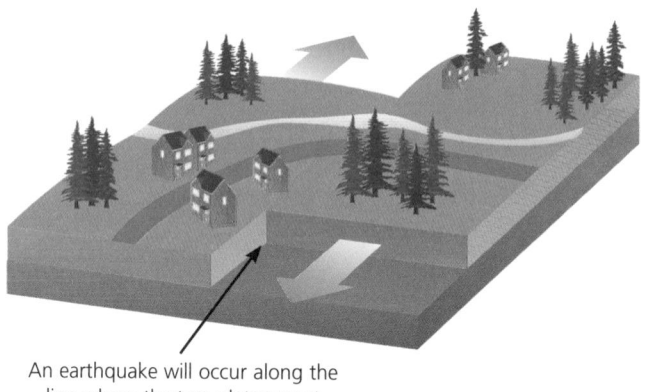

An earthquake will occur along the line where the two plates meet

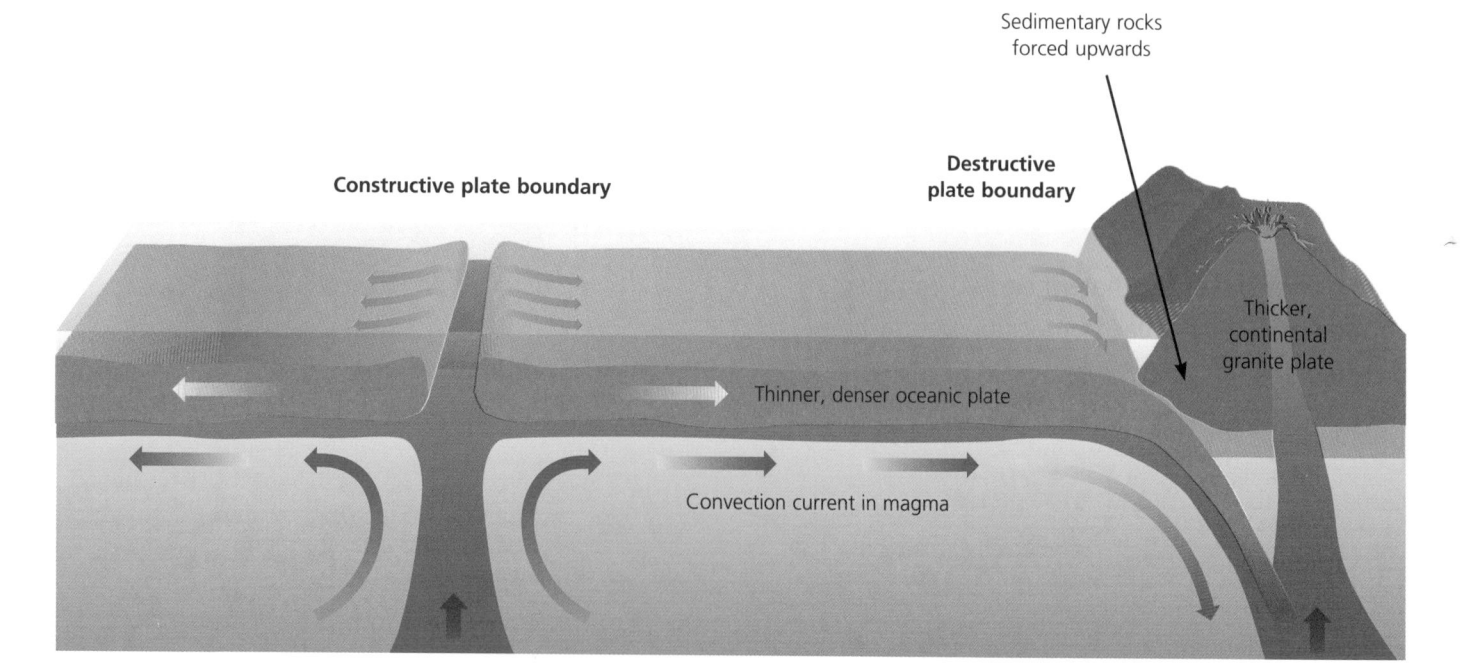

Constructive plate boundary

Destructive plate boundary

Sedimentary rocks forced upwards

Thicker, continental granite plate

Thinner, denser oceanic plate

Convection current in magma

Magma rising and solidifying to form new ocean floor (a few centimetres per year)

Magma rising up through continental crust

Seafloor Spreading

Just below the Earth's crust the mantle is fairly solid. Further down it is liquid and able to move. **Convection currents** in the mantle cause magma (molten rock) to rise to the surface. The force is strong enough to move the solid part of the mantle and the tectonic plates. When the magma reaches the surface, it hardens to form new areas of oceanic crust (seafloor), pushing the existing floor outwards.

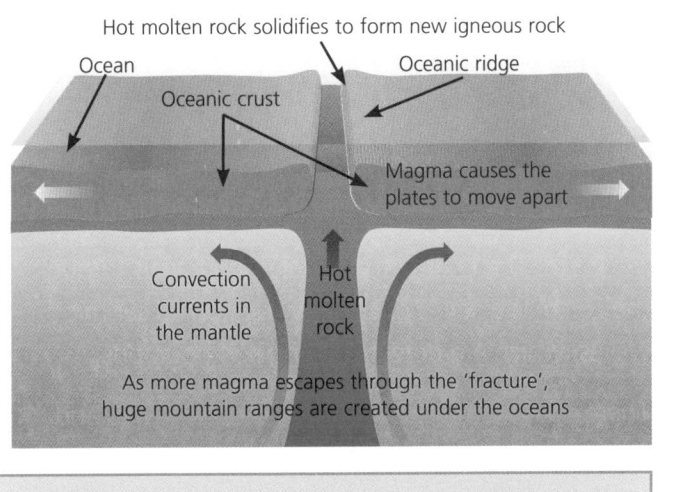

Hot molten rock solidifies to form new igneous rock

Ocean

Oceanic crust

Oceanic ridge

Magma causes the plates to move apart

Convection currents in the mantle

Hot molten rock

As more magma escapes through the 'fracture', huge mountain ranges are created under the oceans

HT Plate Tectonics

New oceanic crust is continuously forming at the crest of an oceanic ridge and old rock is gradually pushed further outwards.

The Earth has a **magnetic field** which changes polarity (reverses) every million years or so. Combined with the spreading of the seafloor, this produces stripes of rock of alternating polarity. Geologists can work out how quickly new crust is forming from the widths of the stripes. This occurs at **constructive plate boundaries**, where the plates are moving apart.

When an oceanic plate and a continental plate collide, the denser oceanic plate is forced under the continental plate. This is called **subduction**. The oceanic plate then melts, and the molten rock can rise upwards to form **volcanoes**. The boundaries where this occurs are called **destructive plate boundaries**.

Mountain ranges form along plate boundaries as sedimentary rock is forced upwards by the pressure created in a collision.

Earthquakes occur most frequently at plate boundaries when plates slide past each other or collide. Pressure builds up over many years due to the force of the plates pushing against each other. Eventually, the stored energy is released in a sudden upheaval of the crust and spreads outwards in waves from the epicentre.

Plate movement plays a crucial role in the **rock cycle**:

- Old rock is destroyed through subduction.
- Igneous rock is formed when magma reaches the surface.
- Plate collisions can produce very high temperatures and pressures, causing the rock to fold and changing sedimentary rock into metamorphic rock.

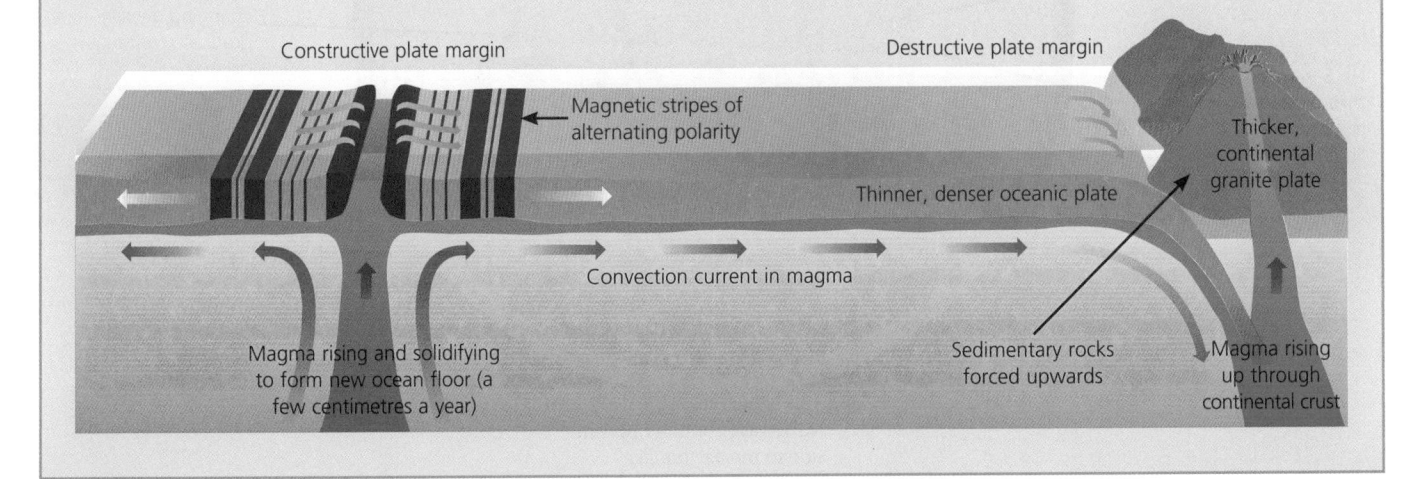

Constructive plate margin

Destructive plate margin

Magnetic stripes of alternating polarity

Thicker, continental granite plate

Thinner, denser oceanic plate

Convection current in magma

Magma rising and solidifying to form new ocean floor (a few centimetres a year)

Sedimentary rocks forced upwards

Magma rising up through continental crust

Evidence for the Structure of the Earth

Evidence for the layered structure of the Earth has been gained through the study of earthquakes. These are due to the fracture of large masses of rock inside the Earth. The energy that is released travels through the Earth as a series of shock waves called seismic waves, which are detected using seismographs.

There are two types of shock waves: P-waves and S-waves. Differences in the speed of P- and S-waves can be used to give evidence for the structure of the Earth.

P-waves

> **HT**
> - Longitudinal (see page 67) waves where the ground is made to vibrate in the same direction as the shock wave is travelling, i.e. if the shock wave is travelling from left to right the ground also vibrates from left to right.

- Pass through solids and liquids.
- Faster than S-waves.
- Speed increases in denser material.

S-waves

> **HT**
> - Transverse waves (see page 67) where the ground is made to vibrate at right angles to the direction the shock wave is travelling, i.e. if the shock wave is travelling from left to right the ground vibrates up and down.

- Pass through solids only.
- Slower than P-waves.
- Speed increases in denser material.

P-waves – building vibrates left to right

S-waves – building vibrates up and down

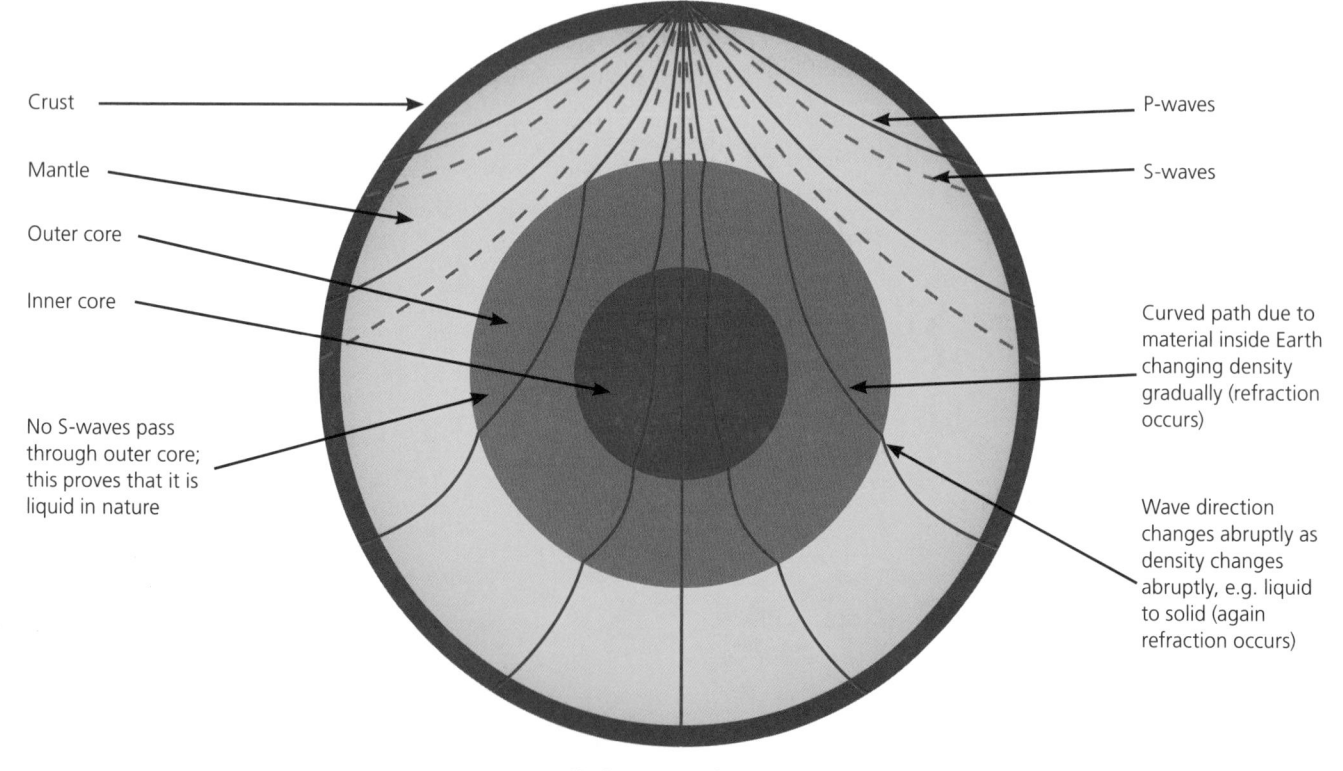

Earthquake

Crust

Mantle

Outer core

Inner core

P-waves

S-waves

Curved path due to material inside Earth changing density gradually (refraction occurs)

Wave direction changes abruptly as density changes abruptly, e.g. liquid to solid (again refraction occurs)

No S-waves pass through outer core; this proves that it is liquid in nature

No S-waves on the opposite side to the earthquake

Types of Waves

Waves are regular patterns of disturbance that transfer energy in the direction the wave travels without transferring matter. There are two types of wave – **longitudinal** and **transverse**.

All waves transfer energy from one point to another without transferring particles of matter. If we consider that each coil of the slinky spring in the following diagrams represents one particle, then we can show the movement of the particles in each type of wave.

Longitudinal Waves

Each particle moves backwards and forwards in the same plane as the direction of wave movement. Each particle simply vibrates to and fro about its normal position.

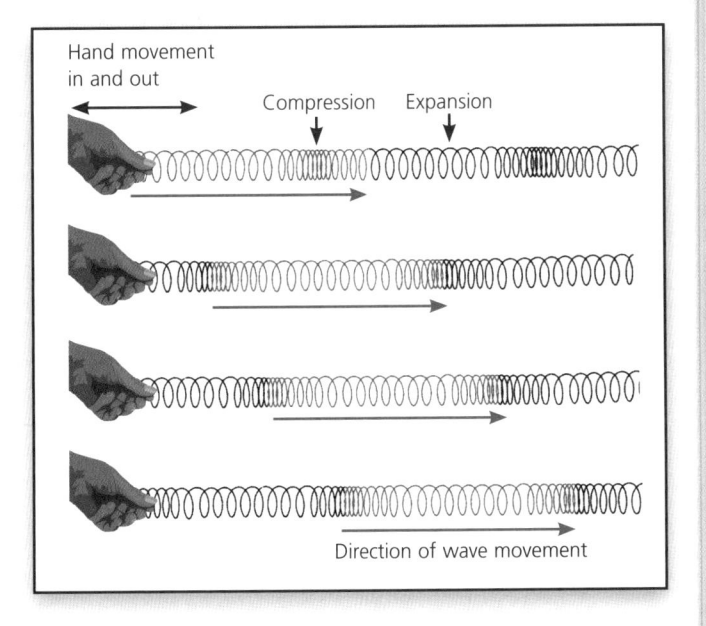

Sound travels as longitudinal waves.

Transverse Waves

Each particle moves up and down at right angles (90°) to the direction of wave movement. Each particle simply vibrates up and down about its normal position.

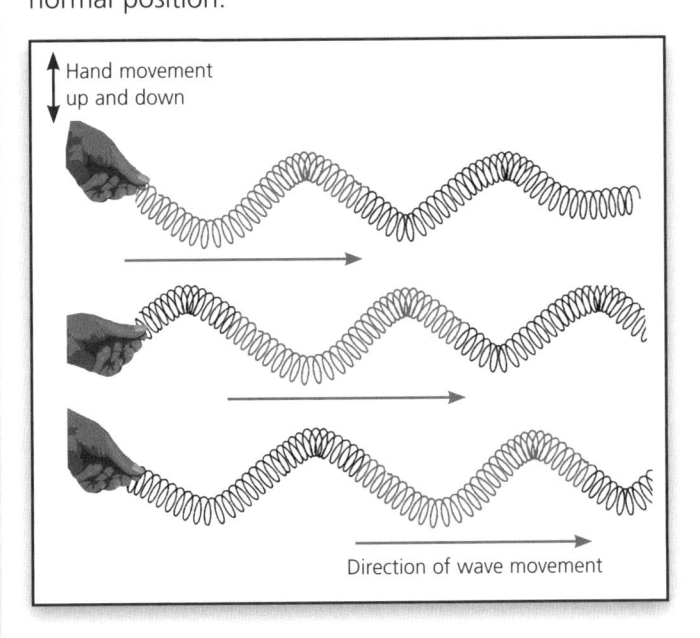

Light and water ripples both travel as transverse waves.

Distance Travelled by a Wave

The distance travelled by a wave can be worked out using the formula:

Distance (metres, m)	=	Wave speed (metres per second, m/s)	×	Time (seconds, s)

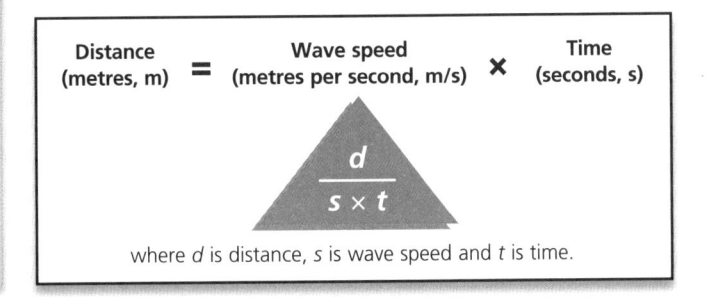

where d is distance, s is wave speed and t is time.

Wave Features

All waves have several important features:

- **Amplitude** – the maximum disturbance caused by a wave. It is measured by the distance from a crest or trough of the wave to the undisturbed position.
- **Wavelength** – the distance between corresponding points on two adjacent disturbances.
- **Frequency** – the number of waves produced, (or passing a particular point) in one second. Frequency is measured in hertz (Hz).

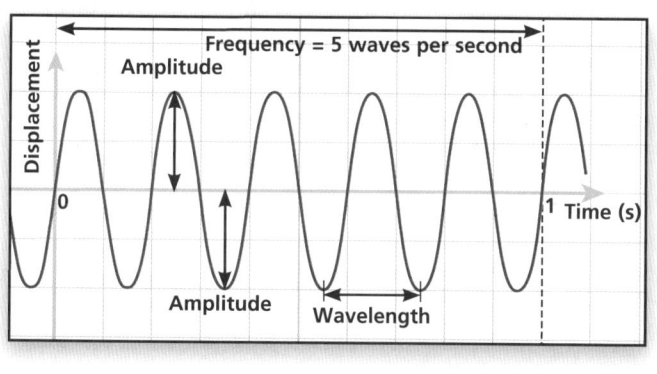

Wave Speed, Wavelength and Frequency

If a wave travels at a **constant speed** (i.e. its speed does not change), then:

- increasing its frequency will decrease its wavelength
- decreasing its frequency will increase its wavelength.

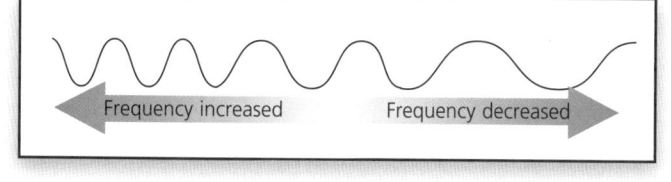

If a wave has a **constant frequency** (i.e. its frequency does not change), then:

- decreasing its wave speed will decrease its wavelength
- increasing its wave speed will increase its wavelength.

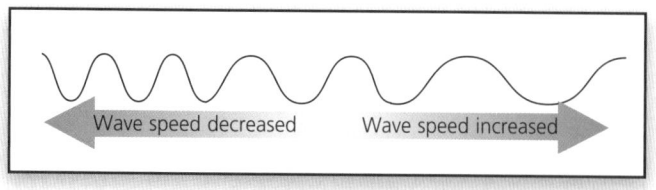

N.B. The speed of a wave is usually independent of its frequency and amplitude.

The Wave Equation

Wave speed, frequency and wavelength are related by the following formula:

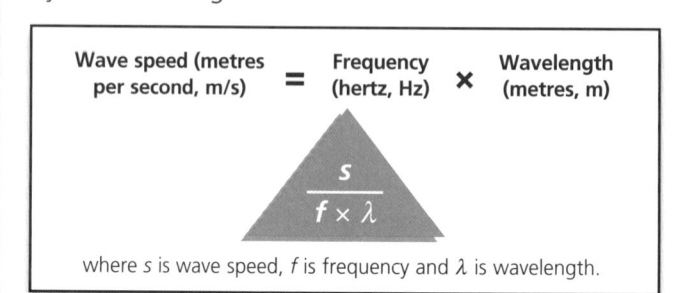

where s is wave speed, f is frequency and λ is wavelength.

For a constant wave speed, the wavelength is inversely proportional to the frequency.

Example

A tapped tuning fork of frequency 480Hz produces sound waves with a wavelength of 70cm. What is the speed of the wave?

Using our relationship:

Wave speed = Frequency × Wavelength

= 480Hz × 0.7m ← *Wavelength must be in metres.*

= **336m/s**

HT The wave speed formula can be rearranged using the formula triangle to work out the frequency or wavelength.

Example

Radio 5 Live transmits on a frequency of 909 000Hz. If the speed of radio waves is 300 000 000m/s, on what wavelength does it transmit?

Rearrange the formula:

Wave speed = Frequency × Wavelength

$$\text{Wavelength} = \frac{\text{Wave speed}}{\text{Frequency}}$$

$$= \frac{300\,000\,000\text{m/s}}{909\,000\text{Hz}} = \textbf{330m}$$

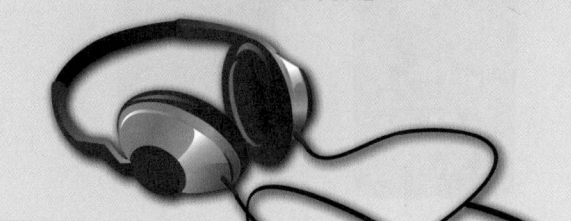

Module P2 (Radiation and Life)

Radiation is all around us and, while there are some dangers and hazards, certain radiations are essential to life on this planet. This module looks at:

- the electromagnetic spectrum
- how radiation is transmitted
- ionising radiation and any harmful effects
- what happens to sunlight entering the Earth's atmosphere
- the carbon cycle and evidence of global warming
- how information is added to a wave.

The Electromagnetic Spectrum

The electromagnetic spectrum is a family of seven **radiations**, including visible light.

A beam of electromagnetic radiation contains 'packets' of energy called **photons**. Different radiations contain photons that carry different amounts of energy.

The intensity of a beam of radiation depends on the number of these **photons** it delivers every second. The intensity of the beam also depends upon the amount of energy carried by each photon.

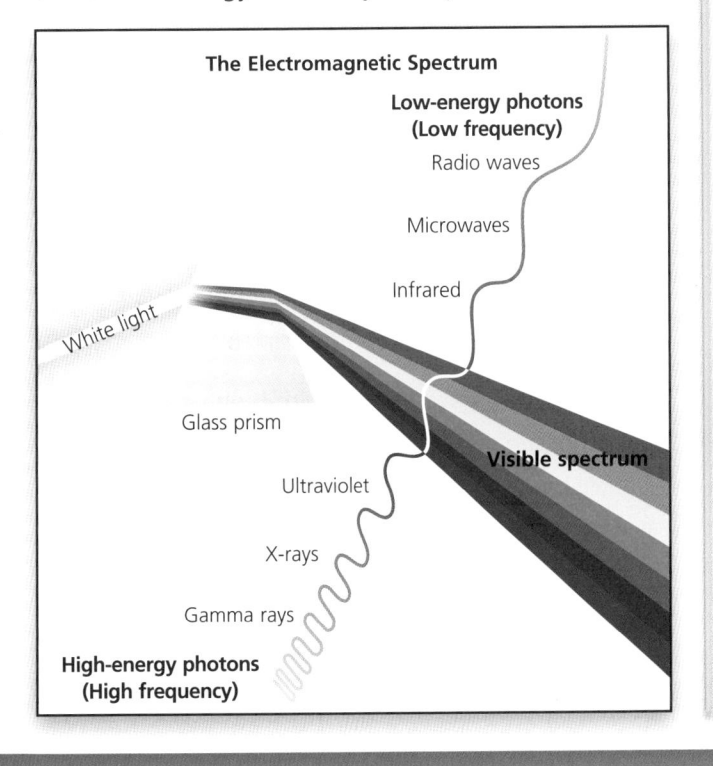

The Electromagnetic Spectrum

Low-energy photons (Low frequency)

Radio waves

Microwaves

Infrared

White light

Glass prism

Visible spectrum

Ultraviolet

X-rays

Gamma rays

High-energy photons (High frequency)

The higher the frequency of the electromagnetic radiation, the more energy is transferred by each photon.

Transmitting Radiation

All electromagnetic waves travel through space (a vacuum) at the same very high speed (300 000 km/s).

A general model of radiation describes how energy travels from a source that emits radiation to a detector that absorbs radiation.

Examples

Emitter	How Waves Travel	Detector
TV transmitter	Radio waves	TV aerial
Mobile phone mast	Microwaves	Mobile phones
The Sun	Light	The eye
Remote control	Infrared	Television
Some stars (e.g. supernova)	Gamma rays	Gamma-ray telescope
X-ray machine	X-rays	Photographic plate

On the journey from emitter to detector the radiation can be transmitted, reflected or absorbed by materials. For example, on a cloudy day energy from the Sun is absorbed and reflected by the clouds, and the amount of light received at the ground is less than it would be on a sunny day.

Intensity and Heat

The **intensity** (or measure of strength) of electromagnetic radiation is the **energy** arriving at a **square metre** of surface **per second**.

The intensity depends on the number of photons delivered per second and the amount of energy each individual packet contains, i.e. the photon energy.

The intensity of a beam of radiation decreases with distance, so the further away from a source you are, the lower the intensity.

HT This decrease in intensity is due to three factors:

- The photons spread out as they travel so the energy is more spread out.
- Some of the photons are absorbed by particles in the substances they pass through.
- Some of the photons are reflected and scattered by other particles.

These effects combine to reduce the number of photons arriving per second at a detector, resulting in a lower measured intensity.

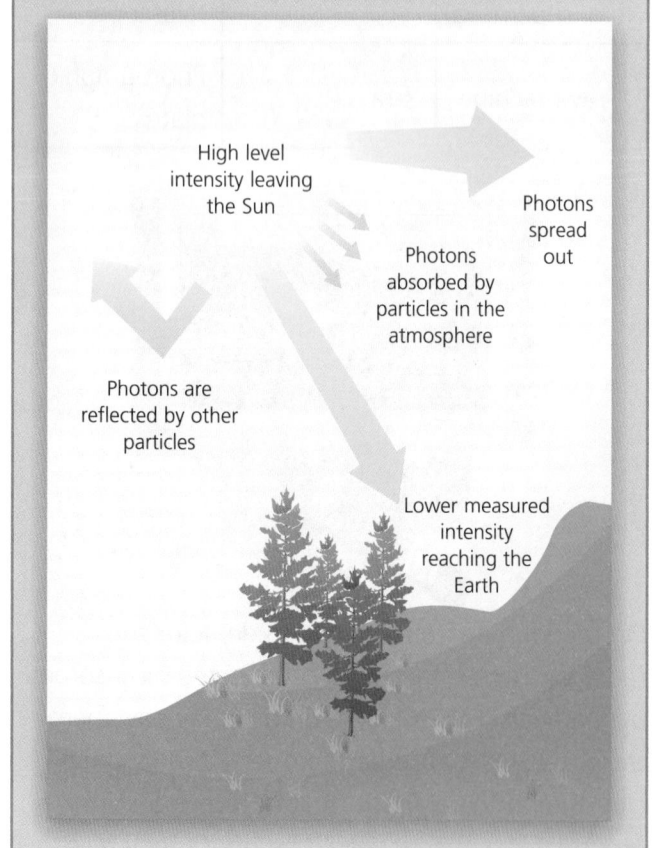

High level intensity leaving the Sun

Photons spread out

Photons absorbed by particles in the atmosphere

Photons are reflected by other particles

Lower measured intensity reaching the Earth

When a material absorbs radiation, it will heat up; the temperature increase depends on the intensity of the radiation.

The amount of heating also depends on the duration of exposure.

Some electromagnetic radiations (ultraviolet, X-rays, gamma rays) have enough energy to change atoms or molecules.

HT These changes can initiate a chemical reaction.

Ionising Radiation

Some materials (radioactive materials) emit ionising gamma radiation all the time. Ionising radiation has photons with enough energy to remove an electron from an atom or molecule to form **ions**.

Ionising radiations are those with high enough photon energy to remove an electron from an atom or molecule. Ultraviolet radiation, X-rays and gamma rays are all examples of ionising radiation.

HT Ions are very reactive and can easily take part in other chemical reactions.

Cell Damage

When living cells absorb radiation, damage can occur in different ways:

- The heating effect can cause damage.
- Ionising radiation, such as ultraviolet radiation, can damage cells, causing ageing of the skin.
- Ionising radiation can cause mutations in the nucleus of a cell, which can lead to cancer.
- Different amounts of exposure can cause different effects, e.g. high-intensity ionising radiation can kill cells, leading to radiation poisoning.

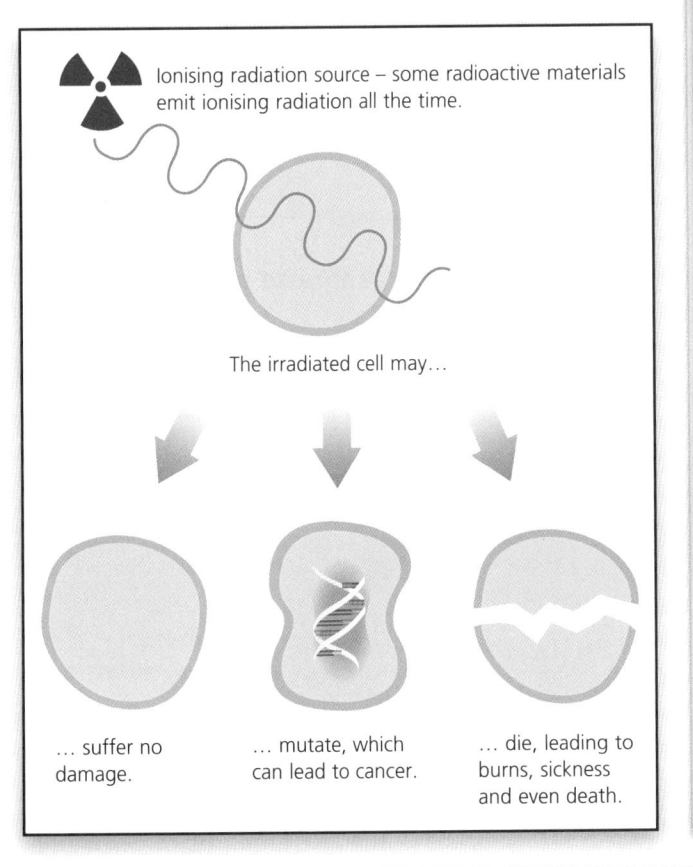

Ionising radiation source – some radioactive materials emit ionising radiation all the time.

The irradiated cell may...

... suffer no damage.

... mutate, which can lead to cancer.

... die, leading to burns, sickness and even death.

Radiation Protection

Microwaves are strongly absorbed by water molecules, which means microwaves can be used to heat objects containing water.

Microwave ovens have a metal case and a wire screen in the door – this reflects the microwaves and protects users by preventing too much radiation from escaping. The door screen also absorbs microwaves, protecting users from the radiation.

There may be a health risk from the low-intensity microwaves of mobile phone handsets and masts, but this is disputed. A study in 2005 found no link from short-term use, but other studies have found some correlation between mobile phone masts and health problems. Further studies are underway to look in more detail at mobile phone masts and the long-term effects of mobile phone use.

Other physical barriers are used to protect people from ionising radiation, e.g. sun-screens and clothing can absorb most of the ultraviolet radiation from the Sun, and this helps to prevent skin cancer.

Using Absorption

X-rays are absorbed by dense materials, so they can be used to produce shadow pictures of bones in our bodies or of objects in aircraft passengers' luggage. Radiographers are protected from radiation by dense materials such as lead and concrete.

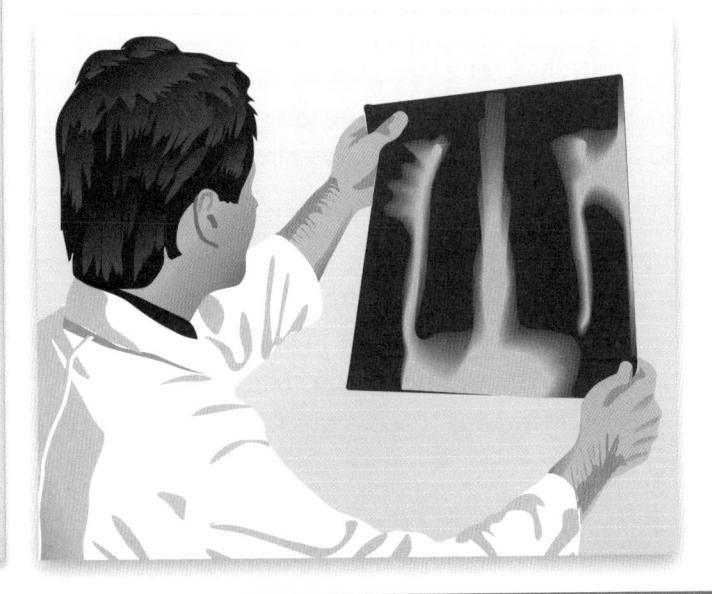

The Sun's Energy

The Sun (and all other objects) emits electromagnetic radiation with a principal frequency that increases with temperature. The Earth is surrounded by an atmosphere that allows some of the electromagnetic radiation emitted by the Sun to pass through.

This radiation warms the surface of the Earth when it is absorbed.

The Ozone Layer

The ozone layer is a thin layer of gas in the Earth's upper atmosphere. This layer of gas absorbs some of the ultraviolet radiation from the Sun before it can reach Earth.

Without the ozone layer, the amount of ultraviolet radiation reaching Earth would be very harmful to living organisms, especially animals, due to cell damage.

> **HT** The energy from the ultraviolet radiation causes chemical changes in the upper atmosphere when it is absorbed by the ozone layer, but these changes are reversible.

The Greenhouse Effect

The Earth emits electromagnetic radiation into space.

> **HT** This radiation has a lower principal frequency than that emitted by the Sun.

There are gases in the atmosphere that absorb or reflect some of this radiation. This keeps the Earth warmer than it would otherwise be and is known as the **greenhouse effect**.

Greenhouse Gases

Carbon dioxide is a **greenhouse gas** and it makes up a small amount of the Earth's atmosphere – about 0.035%. Other greenhouse gases include water vapour and very small amounts of methane.

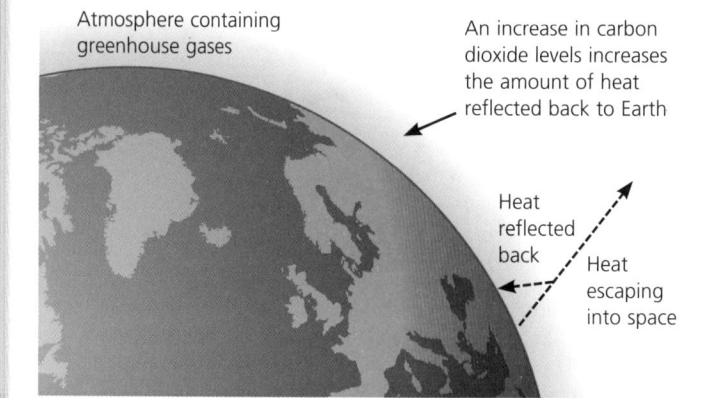

Atmosphere containing greenhouse gases

An increase in carbon dioxide levels increases the amount of heat reflected back to Earth

Heat reflected back

Heat escaping into space

The Carbon Cycle

The carbon cycle is an example of a balanced system.

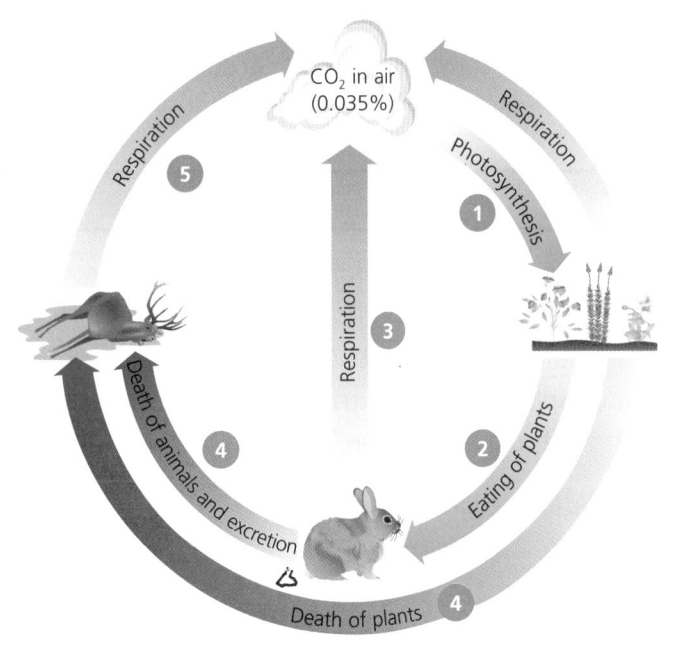

1. Carbon dioxide is removed from the atmosphere by green plants to produce glucose by photosynthesis. Some is returned to the atmosphere by the plants during respiration.
2. The carbon obtained by photosynthesis is used to make carbohydrates, fats and proteins in plants. When the plants are eaten by animals, this carbon becomes carbohydrates, fats and proteins in animals.
3. Animals respire, releasing carbon dioxide into the atmosphere.
4. When plants and animals die, other animals and microorganisms feed on their bodies, causing them to break down. Excretion also releases carbon.
5. As the detritus feeders and microorganisms eat the dead plants and animals, they respire, releasing carbon dioxide into the atmosphere.

The carbon cycle can be used to explain several points:
- The amount of **carbon dioxide** in the atmosphere had remained roughly constant for thousands of years because it was constantly being recycled by plants and animals.
- The importance of **decomposers**, which are microorganisms that break down dead material and release carbon dioxide back into the atmosphere.

- The amount of carbon dioxide in the atmosphere has been steadily increasing over the last 200 years, largely due to human activity such as burning fossil fuels and deforestation.
- **Fossil fuels** contain carbon that was removed from the atmosphere millions of years ago and has been 'locked up' ever since. Burning fossil fuels for energy releases this carbon into the atmosphere.
- **Burning forests** (**deforestation**) to clear land not only releases the carbon they contain but also reduces the number of plants removing carbon dioxide from the atmosphere.

Global Warming

The increase of greenhouse gases in the Earth's atmosphere, especially carbon dioxide, means that the amount of absorbed radiation from the Sun also increases. This increases the temperature on Earth, an effect known as global warming. As the Earth becomes hotter, there are some potential results:
- **Climate change** – it may become impossible to grow some food crops in certain areas.
- **Extreme weather conditions** (e.g. floods, droughts, hurricanes).

> **HT** These are caused by increased convection and larger amounts of water vapour in the hotter atmosphere.

- **Rising sea levels** – the melting ice caps and higher ocean temperatures may cause sea levels to rise, which could cause flooding of low-lying land. Some Pacific islands have already been abandoned.

HT Causes of Global Warming

Climatologists collect data about how the Earth's temperature has changed over the years. The data collected is used with climate models to look for patterns. These computer models show that one of the main factors causing global warming is the rise in atmospheric carbon dioxide and other greenhouse gases, providing evidence that human activities are causing global warming.

Uses of Electromagnetic Waves in Communication

Different electromagnetic waves have different frequencies. This affects their properties and the effect that other materials have on them.

They can be used for different purposes, depending on how much they are reflected, absorbed or transmitted by different materials.

Electromagnetic Waves	Properties and Uses
Radio Waves 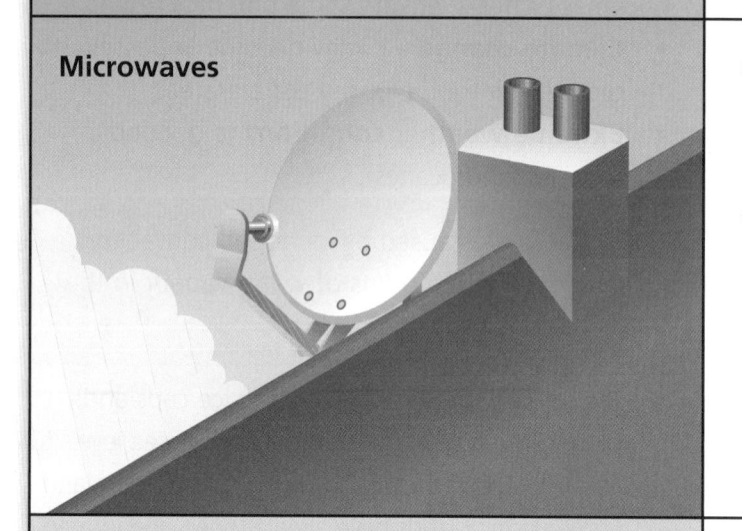	• Radio waves are used for transmitting radio and television programmes because they are not strongly absorbed by the Earth's atmosphere. They can travel long distances through the atmosphere and through space. • Radio telescopes are used in astronomy to pick up radio waves from stars.
Microwaves	• Microwaves are used to transmit mobile phone signals because they are not strongly absorbed by the atmosphere. • They are reflected well by metals so satellite dishes are made of metal and shaped to reflect the signal onto the receiver.
Light and Infrared Radiation	• Light and infrared radiation will travel huge distances down optical fibres without the signal becoming significantly weaker. This makes them very useful for carrying information, e.g. in computer networks and telephone conversations.

Transmitting Information

For communication purposes, information can be superimposed onto an electromagnetic carrier wave, to create a signal.

For a wave to carry a signal, it must be modulated. This involves changing the carrier wave to create a variation that matches the variation in the information that is being transmitted. It is this pattern of variation that carries the information.

The pattern of variation is decoded by the receiver to reproduce the original information, e.g. sound from a radio wave.

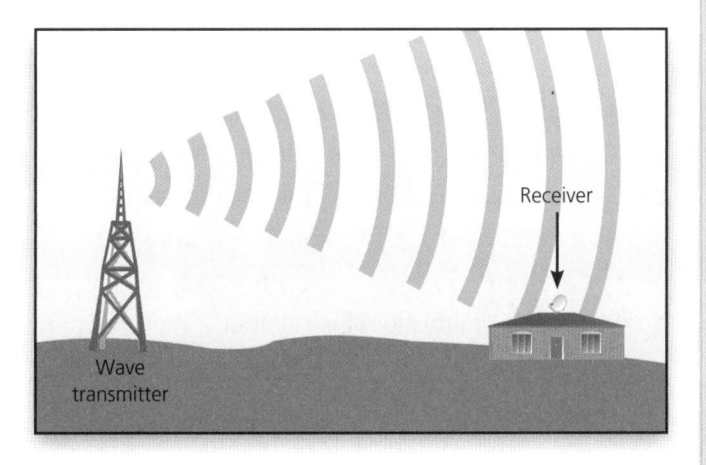

Analogue Signals

An **analogue** signal can vary continuously, so its amplitude and/or frequency can take any value. A sound wave is an example of an analogue signal. Some radio stations are transmitted as analogue signals.

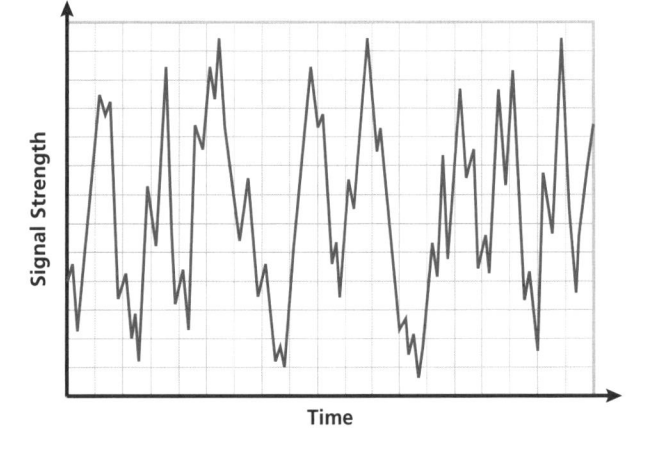

Digital Signals

Information, including sound and images, can also be transmitted digitally. The signal is not sent as a continuously varying transmission. A **digital** signal can only take one of a small number of fixed (discrete) values – usually two. For transmitting information digitally, the digital code is made up of just two symbols, '1' and '0'.

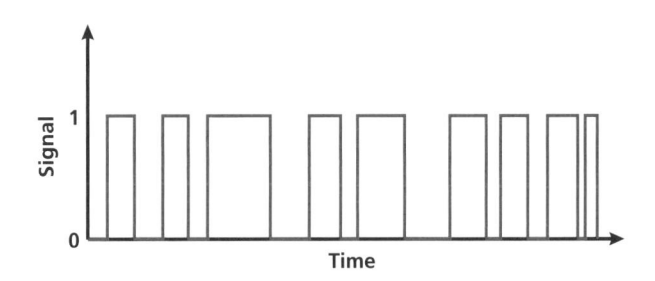

The electromagnetic carrier wave is switched off and on to create short bursts of waves. A receiver decodes the pulses to re-create the original information. Mobile phone signals, digital radio and digital TV are all transmitted in this way.

Benefits of Digital

Both digital and analogue signals become weaker (their amplitude becomes smaller) as they travel. The transmitted signals therefore have to be amplified at selected intervals to make them stronger.

During transmission the signals can also pick up random variations, called **noise**, which reduce the quality of the signal.

With digital signals it is easier to remove the noise, and so recover the original signal. This gives digital signals an important advantage over analogue signals. Information transmitted digitally can travel long distances and is received at a higher quality than analogue signals because any interference can be removed.

Another advantage of using a digital signal is that the information can be stored and processed by computers. Generally, the more information stored (or the more **bytes**, **B**), the higher the quality of the sound or image.

HT Signal Quality

Analogue signals can have many different values, so it is hard to distinguish between noise and the original signal. This means that noise cannot be completely removed and, when the signal is amplified, any noise that has been picked up is also amplified.

With analogue signals you are often left with a noisy signal. With music this can involve a 'hissing' sound.

Digital signals, which have two states, on (1) or off (0), can still be recognised despite any noise that is picked up. Therefore, it is easy to remove the noise and clean up the signal, restoring the on / off pattern. So, when it is amplified, the quality of the digital signal is retained.

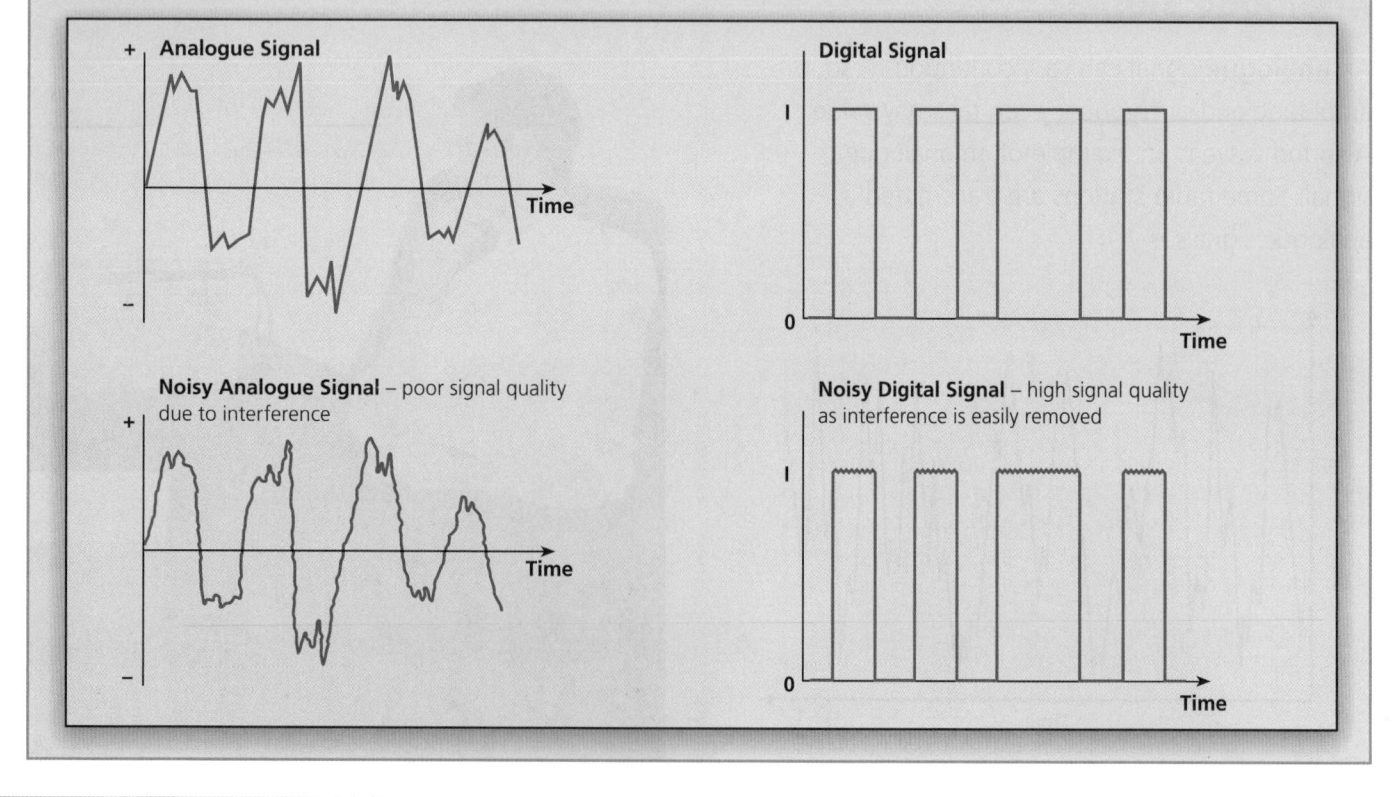

Analogue Signal

Noisy Analogue Signal – poor signal quality due to interference

Digital Signal

Noisy Digital Signal – high signal quality as interference is easily removed

Module P3 (Sustainable Energy)

Energy is generated from a variety of sources and the electricity is used in the home. This module looks at:

- how electricity is generated
- renewable and non-renewable energy sources
- generators and power
- the cost of electricity
- energy efficiency.

Electricity

Electricity is called a **secondary energy source** because it is generated from another energy source, e.g. coal, nuclear, wind, etc.

During the generation process some energy is always lost to the surroundings. This makes electricity less efficient than when compared with using the primary resource directly.

However, the convenience of electricity makes it very useful. It can be easily transmitted over long distances and used in a variety of ways.

Generating Electricity

To generate electricity, fuel (either fossil fuel or nuclear) is used to release energy as heat.

The heat is used to boil water which produces steam, and the steam is then used to drive the turbines that power the generators.

The electricity produced in the generators is sent to a transformer and then to the National Grid. The voltage is then reduced to a safer level of 230V, after which we can access it in our homes.

In a **fossil fuel** power station the fuel is burned to release the chemical energy it contains as heat. As they are burning carbon fuels, the power stations also produce carbon dioxide, a greenhouse gas.

In a **nuclear** power station the energy is released due to changes in the nucleus of radioactive substances. Nuclear power stations do not produce carbon dioxide, but they do produce **radioactive waste**.

Nuclear waste emits ionising radiation, and this can cause a number of health-related issues:

- **Irradiation** means exposure to radiation. This can happen naturally through background radiation from sources such as the Earth or space. It could also happen by exposure during medical treatments such as X-rays. In such cases the cells may become damaged, but the person does not become radioactive. Increased exposure may eventually lead to cancer and death.
- **Contamination** involves a radioactive material being placed inside a person. This can be far more damaging than irradiation, yet it is often used in medical treatments where the risk is considered worth the benefit, such as tumour suppression.

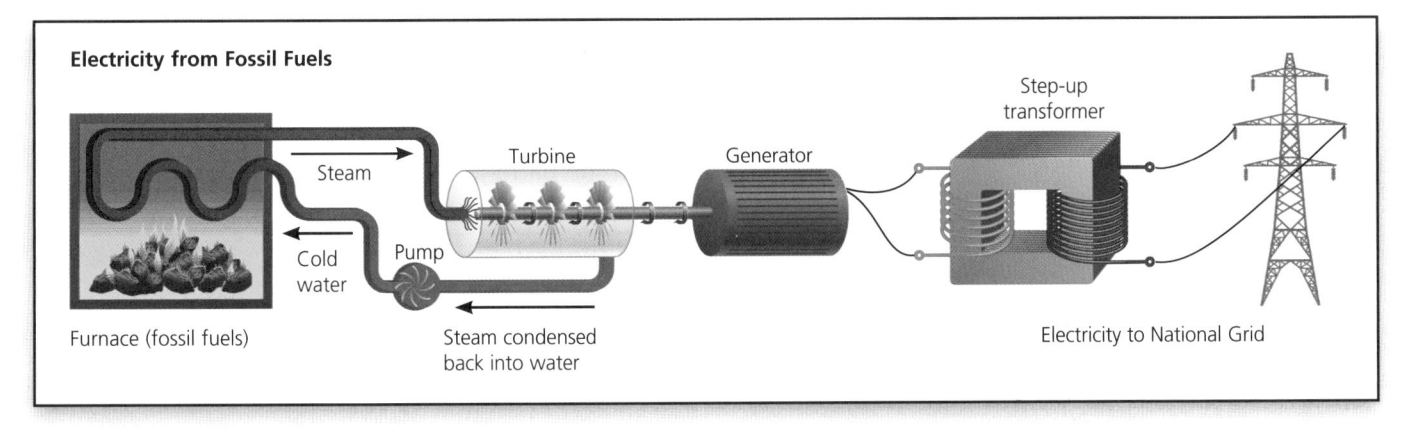

Electricity from Fossil Fuels

Furnace (fossil fuels) · Steam · Cold water · Pump · Steam condensed back into water · Turbine · Generator · Step-up transformer · Electricity to National Grid

Non-renewable Energy Sources

Coal, oil and gas are energy sources that are formed over millions of years from the remains of plants and animals. They are called **fossil fuels** and are responsible for most of the energy that we use. However, because they cannot be replaced within a lifetime, they will eventually run out. They are therefore called **non-renewable** energy sources.

| Coal | Oil | Gas |

Nuclear fuels such as uranium and plutonium are also non-renewable. Nuclear fission is the splitting of a nucleus that generates thousands of times more heat energy than burning the same mass of fossil fuel.

However, nuclear fuel is not burned like coal, oil or gas to release energy and is not classed as a fossil fuel.

Renewable Energy Sources

As the demand for electricity continually increases, other sources of energy are needed. Renewable energy sources are those that will not run out because they are continually being replaced. Many of them are caused by the Sun or Moon. The gravitational pull of the Moon creates tides, and the Sun causes:

- evaporation, which results in rain and flowing water
- convection currents, which result in winds, that in turn create waves.

Generating Electricity from Renewable Energy Sources

Renewable energy sources can be used to drive turbines or generators directly. In other words, no fuel needs to be burned to produce heat.

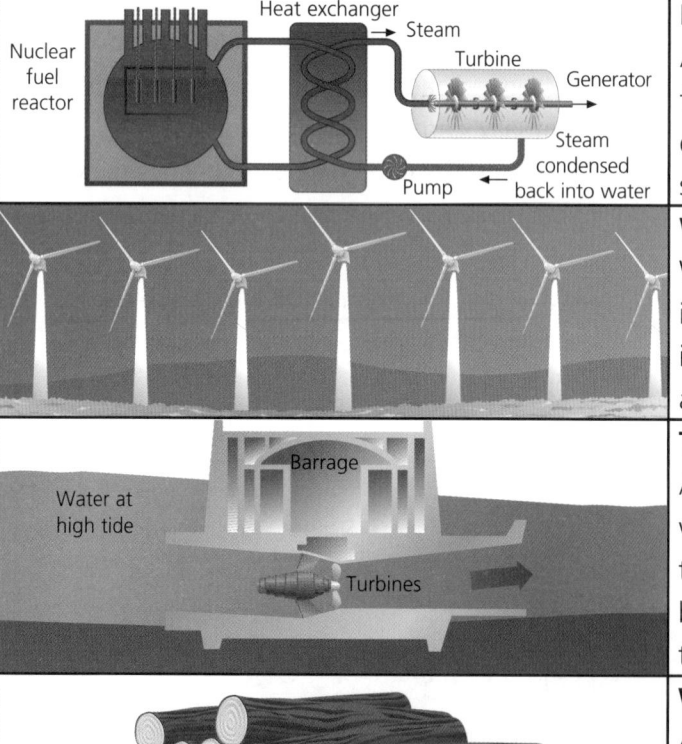

	Nuclear Fuel (Non-renewable) A nuclear reactor is used to generate heat by nuclear fission. A heat exchanger is used to transfer the heat energy from the reactor to the water, which turns to steam and drives the turbines.
	Wind Turbines (Renewable) Wind can be used to drive huge turbines which, in turn, drive generators. Wind turbines are positioned in exposed places where there is a lot of wind, such as the tops of hills or offshore.
	Tidal Barrage (Renewable) As the tide comes in, water flows freely through a valve in the barrage. This water then becomes trapped. At low tide, the water is released from behind the barrage through a gap which has a turbine in it. This drives a generator.
	Wood (Renewable) Although burned for energy, wood is not a fossil fuel, nor is it non-renewable. It is classed as a **renewable** energy source since trees can be grown relatively quickly to replace those that are burned to provide energy for heating.

Comparing Non-renewable Sources of Energy

The energy sources below provide most of the electricity we need in this country through power stations.

Source	Advantages	Disadvantages
Gas	• Enough natural gas left for the short to medium term. • Can be found as easily as oil. • No sulfur dioxide (SO_2) is produced. • Gas-fired power stations are flexible in meeting demand and have a quicker start-up time than nuclear, coal and oil-fired reactors.	• Burning produces carbon dioxide (CO_2), although it produces less than coal and oil per unit of energy. (CO_2 contributes to global warming and climate change.) • Expensive pipelines and networks are often required to transport it to the point of use.
Coal	• Relatively cheap and easy to obtain. • Coal-fired power stations are flexible in meeting demand and have a quicker start-up time than their nuclear equivalents. • Estimates suggest that there may be over a century's worth of coal left.	• Burning produces CO_2 and SO_2. • Produces more CO_2 per unit of energy than oil or gas does. • SO_2 causes acid rain unless the sulfur is removed before burning or the SO_2 is removed from the waste gases. Both of these add to the cost of electricity.
Oil	• Enough oil left for the short to medium term. • Relatively easy to find, though the price is variable. • Oil-fired power stations are flexible in meeting demand and have a quicker start-up time than both nuclear-powered and coal-fired reactors.	• Burning produces CO_2 and SO_2. • Produces more CO_2 than gas per unit of energy. • Often carried between continents on tankers leading to the risk of spillage and pollution.
Nuclear	• Cost of fuel is relatively low. • Nuclear power stations are flexible in meeting demand. • No CO_2 or SO_2 produced.	• Although there is very little escape of radioactive material in normal use, radioactive waste can stay dangerously radioactive for thousands of years and safe storage is expensive. • Building and decommissioning is costly. • Longest comparative start-up time.

Summary of Non-renewable Resources

Advantages	Disadvantages
• Produce huge amounts of energy. • Reliable. • Flexible in meeting demand. • Do not take up much space (relatively).	• Pollute the environment. • Cause global warming and acid rain (fossil fuels only). • Will eventually run out. • Fuels often have to be transported over long distances.

Comparing Renewable Sources of Energy

The energy sources below use modern technology to provide a clean, safe alternative source of energy.

Source	Advantages	Disadvantages
Wind	• No fuel and little maintenance required. • No pollutant gases produced. • Once built, wind turbines provide 'free' energy when the wind is blowing. • Can be built offshore.	• Need a lot to produce a sizeable amount of electricity, which means noise and visual pollution. • Electricity output depends on the wind. • Not very flexible in meeting demand. • Capital outlay can be high to build turbines.
Tidal and Waves	• No fuel required. • No pollutant gases produced. • Once built, installations provide 'free' energy. • Barrage water can be released when demand for electricity is high.	• Tidal barrages across estuaries are unsightly, a hazard to shipping, and destroy the habitats of wading birds, etc. • Daily variations of tides and waves affect output. • High initial capital outlay to build barrages.
Hydro-electric	• No fuel required unless storing energy to meet future demand. • Fast start-up time to meet growing demand. • Produces a lot of clean, reliable electricity. • No pollutant gases produced. • Water can be pumped back up to the reservoir when demand for electricity is low, e.g. in the night.	• Location is critical and often involves damming upland valleys, which means flooding farms, forests and natural habitats. • To achieve a net output (aside from pumping) there must be adequate rainfall in the region where the reservoir is. • Very high initial capital outlay (though worth the investment in the end).
Solar	• Ideal for producing electricity in remote locations. • Excellent energy source for small amounts. • Produces free, clean electricity. • No pollutant gases produced.	• Dependent on the intensity of light. • High cost per unit of electricity produced, compared to all other sources except non-rechargeable batteries.
Bio-fuels	• Contain no sulfur (responsible for acid rain). • Can use many readily available waste materials. • Could be considered carbon neutral.	• Have lower energy output than traditional fuels. • Could lead to competition of land use between fuel and food.
Geo-thermal	• Minimal fuel costs. • Long life span and varying size of power output.	• High initial capital costs. • Possible environmental damage from harmful gases escaping from deep within the Earth.

Summary of Renewable Sources

Advantages	Disadvantages
• No fuel costs during operation. • Generally no chemical pollution. • Often low maintenance.	• Some produce small amounts of electricity. • Can be unreliable. • High initial capital outlay for most.

HT You may be asked to interpret and evaluate information about different energy sources for generating electricity, considering power output and lifetime.

The Electric Generator

Mains electricity is produced by generators. Generators use the principle of electromagnetic induction to generate electricity by rotating a magnet inside a coil.

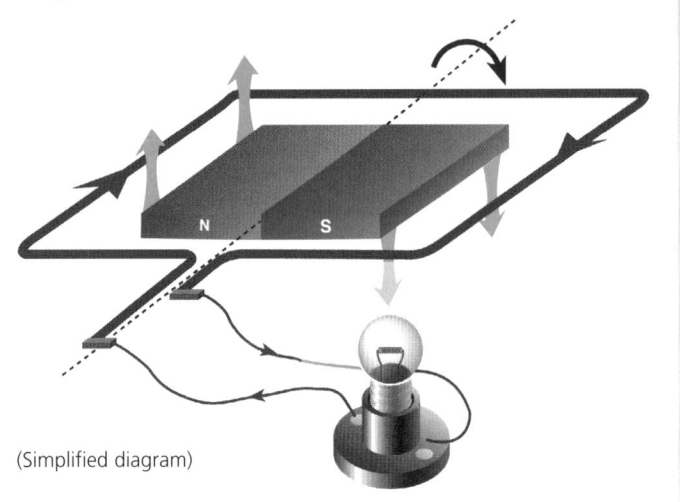

(Simplified diagram)

Power

When charge flows through a component, energy is transferred to the component. Power, measured in watts (W), is a measure of how much energy is transferred every second.

HT Power is therefore **the rate of energy transfer**.

Electrical power can be calculated using the following equation:

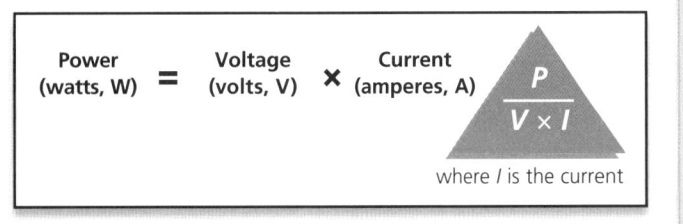

$$\text{Power (watts, W)} = \text{Voltage (volts, V)} \times \text{Current (amperes, A)}$$

$$\frac{P}{V \times I}$$

where *I* is the current

Example

A hairdryer has a current of 3A and a potential difference of 230V. What is the power of the hairdryer?

$$
\begin{aligned}
\text{Power} &= \text{Voltage} \times \text{Current} \\
&= 230V \times 3A \\
&= \textbf{690W}
\end{aligned}
$$

HT The power formula can be rearranged using the formula triangle to work out the potential difference or current.

Example

What current is needed to power a 6W light bulb with a potential difference of 3V?

$$
\begin{aligned}
\text{Current} &= \frac{\text{Power}}{\text{Voltage}} \\
&= \frac{6W}{3V} \\
&= \textbf{2A}
\end{aligned}
$$

Energy

Energy is measured in joules (J). A joule is a very small amount of energy, so a domestic electricity meter measures the energy transfer in a much larger unit, the kilowatt hour (kWh).

The amount of energy transferred for either joules or kilowatt hours can be calculated by the following equation:

| Energy transferred (joules, J) | = | Power (watts, W) | × | Time (seconds, s) |
| Energy transferred (kilowatt hours, kWh) | = | Power (kilowatts, kW) | × | Time (hours, h) |

$$\frac{E}{P \times t}$$

Examples

1. A 30W light bulb is switched on for 45 seconds. What is the energy transferred in joules?

   Energy transferred = Power × Time
   = 30W × 45s
   = **1350J**

2. A 2000W electric hot plate is switched on for 90 minutes. What is the energy transferred in kilowatt hours?

   Energy transferred = 2kW × 1.5h ← Power in kW and time in hours
   = **3kWh**

HT The energy transfer formula can be rearranged using the formula triangle to work out power or time.

Example
A hairdryer is switched on for six minutes and the total energy transferred is 0.2kWh. What is the power rating of the hairdryer?

$$\text{Power} = \frac{\text{Energy transferred}}{\text{Time}} = \frac{0.2kWh}{0.1h} = \textbf{2kW}$$

Cost of Electricity

The cost of the electrical energy used can be calculated if the power, time and cost per kilowatt hour are known.

The formula for the cost of energy is as follows:

| Total cost | = | Number of kWh | × | Cost per kWh |

Example
A 2000W electric fire is switched on for 30 minutes. How much does it cost if electricity is 8p per kWh?

Energy transferred = 2kW × 0.5h
= 1kWh

Cost = 1kWh × 8p
= **8 pence**

Efficiency of Appliances

The greater the proportion of energy that is usefully transferred, the more efficient we say an appliance is. Efficiency can be calculated using the following formula:

$$\text{Efficiency (\%)} = \frac{\text{Energy usefully transferred}}{\text{Total energy supplied}} \times 100\%$$

Examples

Electrical Appliance	Energy In	Useful Energy Out	Efficiency
Light bulb	100 joules/s	Light: 20 joules/s	$\frac{20}{100} \times 100\%$ = **20%** or **0.2**
Kettle	2000 joules/s	Heat (in water): 1800 joules/s	$\frac{1800}{2000} \times 100\%$ = **90%** or **0.9**
Electric motor	500 joules/s	Kinetic: 300 joules/s	$\frac{300}{500} \times 100\%$ = **60%** or **0.6**
Television	200 joules/s	Light: 20 joules/s Sound: 30 joules/s	$\frac{50}{200} \times 100\%$ = **25%** or **0.25**

Losing Energy

Energy is lost at every stage of the process of electricity generation. **Sankey diagrams** can be used to show the generation and distribution of electricity, including the efficiency of energy transfers.

The diagram below shows that of the energy put into the power station, almost half is lost to the surroundings (mostly as heat) before the electricity even reaches the home. When energy passes through any electrical component or device, energy will either be transferred to the device or to the environment.

Further energy is lost during energy transfers in the home when the electricity is used.

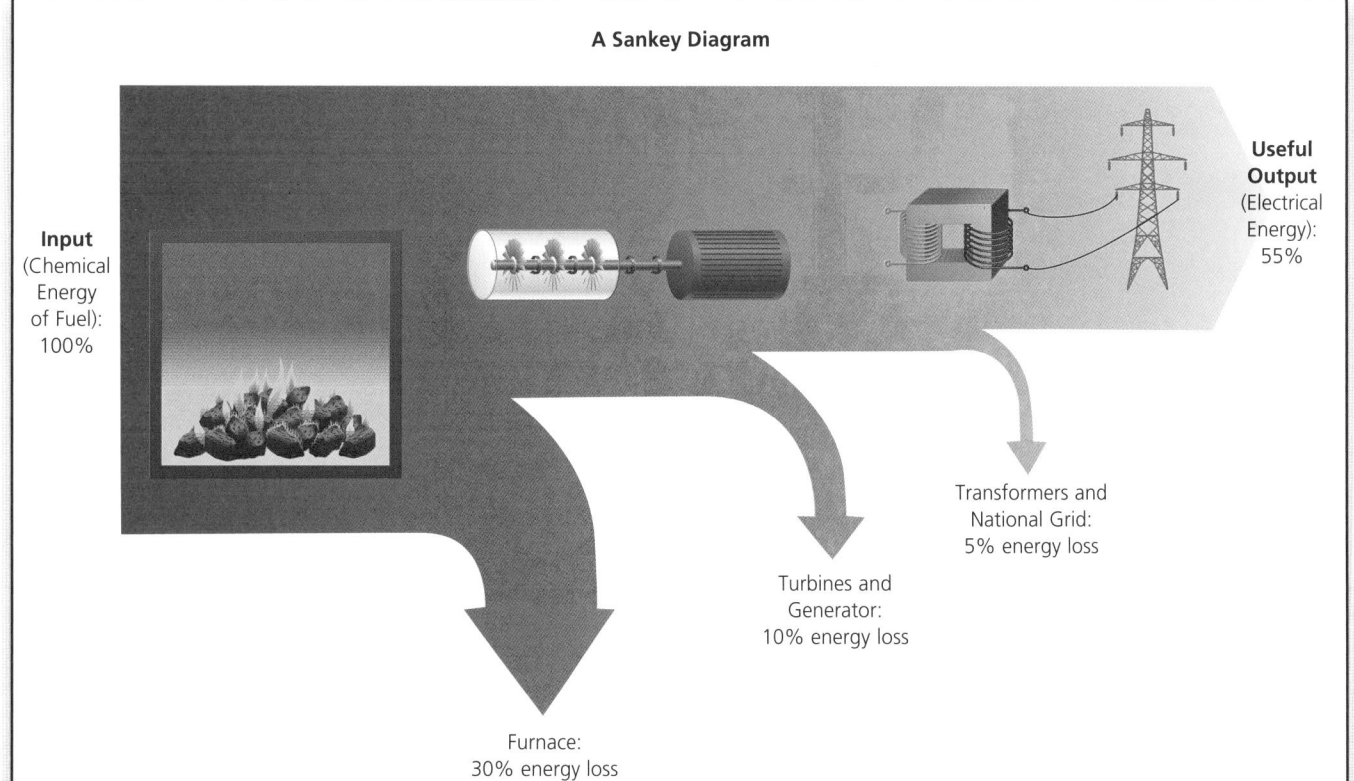

A Sankey Diagram

Input (Chemical Energy of Fuel): 100%

Useful Output (Electrical Energy): 55%

Transformers and National Grid: 5% energy loss

Turbines and Generator: 10% energy loss

Furnace: 30% energy loss

The National Grid

The greater the power supplied by a generator, the more of the primary fuel (coal, oil, etc.) it uses every second. Depending on the type of power station, voltages of between 1000 and 25 000V can be produced.

Due to the inefficiency of electrical energy transfer through cables, the National Grid uses extremely high voltages through its network of pylons. Over half a million volts is often used, meaning a low current is needed and less energy is lost due to heat. The voltages are then reduced to 230V by **transformers** in local substations before safely entering the home.

The Domestic Home

Energy saving in the home can be done in a variety of ways. These include loft insulation, double glazing, draught proofing, lagging the hot water tank and the use of efficient light bulbs.

When considering which methods to employ, the homeowner needs to weigh up the economic effectiveness of any changes.

For example, if you install energy-efficient, double-glazed windows and loft insulation, then when it's time to replace your boiler and heating system, you may be able to manage with a smaller one that costs less. This is because the windows and walls will retain the heated air inside better than a home without efficient windows and insulation.

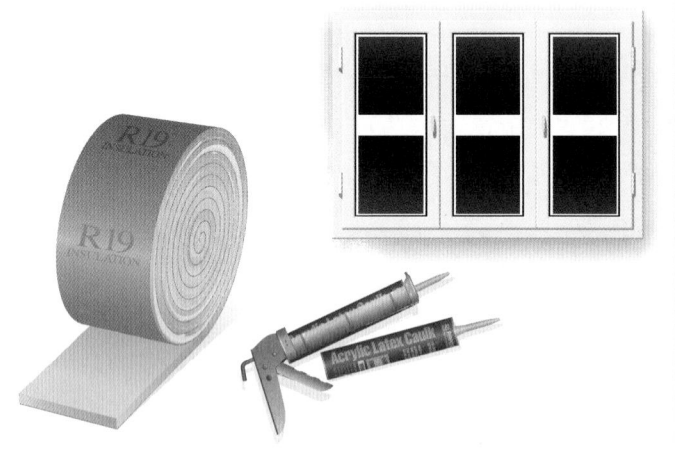

The National Picture

When it comes to saving energy, choices are being made on a national scale as well as domestically. Reducing a country's carbon emissions is quickly becoming a global issue with international agreements such as the Kyoto Protocol.

> **HT** The need to reduce energy usage is important, but so is the need to maintain a secure supply of energy. This is done by using a wide mix of energy sources across the renewable and non-renewable range.

The Workplace

As well as energy loss through the physical infrastructure of a building, a large amount of energy can be saved by following a few simple steps in the workplace.

Turning off computers at the end of the working day, turning down an office radiator by just one degree Celsius or designing spaces to use more natural light can save money and help to reduce the business's carbon footprint.

Ways to Save Energy

In the Home	In the Workplace	National Context
• More efficient appliances, e.g. a condensing boiler could save £190 per year	• Cleaning air conditioner filters – can save 5% of the energy used in running the system	• Replacing old houses with new efficient ones
• Double glazing – possible savings of £130 per year	• Using low-energy light bulbs	• Increased use of public transport
• Loft insulation – possible savings of £145 per year	• Roof insulation / cavity wall insulation in modern buildings	• More efficient trains and buses
• Cavity wall insulation – possible savings of £110 per year	• Use of efficient modern, low-energy machinery	• Encourage more widespread recycling
• Draught-proof rooms – possible savings of £25 per year	• Use of modern, efficient vehicles for transport of goods	• Encourage car sharing and fewer journeys

P1 **1** Studying the solar system around us has helped scientists have a much greater understanding of the Earth and its existence in the Universe.

(a) Place the following in order from smallest to largest:

A The Earth	**B** The Sun	**C** The Moon
D The solar system	**E** The Universe	**F** The galaxy	**[5]**

Smallest							Largest

(b) Approximately how old do scientists believe our solar system to be? **[1]**

(c) What is the speed of light? **[1]**

(d) What is a light-year? **[1]**

P2 **2** The electromagnetic spectrum has many uses, both good and bad.

(a) Complete the table below to show the electromagnetic spectrum in order of low-energy photons to high-energy photons. Choose words from this list:

Ultraviolet   Radio waves   Gamma rays   Infrared

Low-energy photons		Microwaves		Visible spectrum		X-rays		High-energy photons

[3]

(b) When living cells absorb radiation, damage can occur in a number of different ways. List some of the harmful effects of sunbathing. **[3]**

(c) Which parts of the electromagnetic spectrum are ionising and what does ionising mean? **[4]**

P3 **3** Electricity can be generated using a number of different energy resources, some of which are controversial.

(a) What is a **renewable** energy resource? [1]

(b) What is a **non-renewable** energy resource? [1]

(c) Which of the following energy resources are renewable? Put ticks (✓) in the boxes next to the three correct answers. [3]

☐ Coal ☑ Wind ☑ Wood ☒ Natural gas ☐ Oil ☑ Tidal water

(d) The burning of fossil fuels in power stations can cause a number of environmental issues. Explain how burning fossil fuels can lead to climate change. [6]

✎ *The quality of written communication will be assessed in your answer to this question.*

(e) Calculate the amount of energy transferred by a 2000W kettle, when heating up water to make a cup of tea, in one minute. Use the following equation:

Energy transferred (J) = Power (W) × Time (s)

[2]

P1 **4** What is **redshift** and what does it tell us about the Universe? [2]

P1 **5** The Earth's crust has been constantly changing over millions of years, leaving a variety of evidence for scientists to study.

(a) Use the theory of plate tectonics to explain how earthquakes are produced. [4]

(b) Explain why we have magnetic stripes of alternating polarity on either side of the Mid-Atlantic Ridge. [6]

✎ *The quality of written communication will be assessed in your answer to this question.*

(c) By how much does the seafloor spread each year at the Mid-Atlantic Ridge? [1]

Modules B1–B3 (Pages 30–31)

1. (a) DD and Dd should be ticked. [Both must be correct for 1 mark.]

   (b)

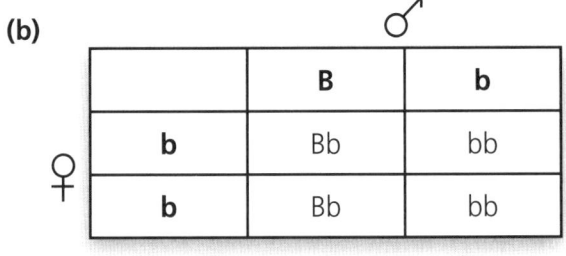

		B	b
	b	Bb	bb
	b	Bb	bb

   [1 mark for the correct pairs of alleles in a column (2 marks in total).]

2. (a) Thick mucus in lungs; Chest infections; **and** Breathing difficulties **should be ticked.**

   (b) **This is a model answer which would score full marks:** Huntington's disease is an incurable genetic disorder that causes suffering. However, people with the condition do not develop it until later life. It would be unethical to abort a fetus carrying the disorder as it could lead a normal life if allowed to develop as normal. Another issue is that the genetic test may be incorrect, giving a false positive, and a healthy fetus could then be aborted.

3. Excessive hunting [1] and removal of habitats [1].

4.

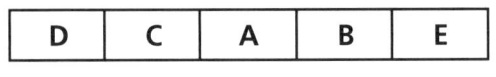

D	C	A	B	E

   [2 marks for all five; 1 mark for three]

5. **This is a model answer which would score full marks:** Genetic testing is not 100% accurate. A false positive would lead to a person worrying about a condition they do not have, whilst a false negative would mean that a carrier does not avoid lifestyle factors that could trigger the disorder. Some disorders are incurable and, therefore, knowing about it in advance is not going to help. Companies could also get hold of the results, which may mean a carrier cannot get a job or life insurance.

6.

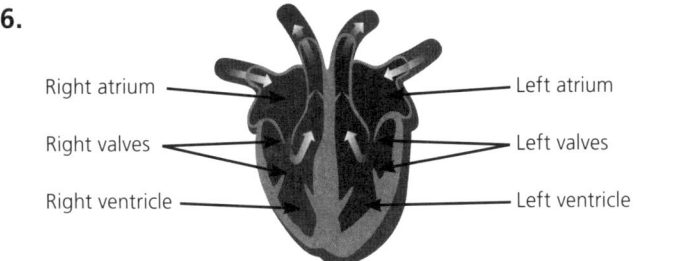

[1 mark for each correct pair of labels.]

7. Genotype – The alleles present for a gene in an individual
   Phenotype – The characteristics expressed in the environment
   Allele – A version of a gene
   Heterozygous – Possessing one of each allele type
   Homozygous – Possessing two of the same alleles

8. Enough of the population is vaccinated to avoid an epidemic **should be ticked.**

9. 10%

Answers

Modules C1–C3 (Pages 56–57)

1. (a)

B	A	D	E	C

   [1 mark if one correct, 2 marks if two correct, 3 marks if all correct.]

   (b) C **should be ticked.**

   (c) **This is a model answer which would score full marks:** Carbon dioxide levels are increasing. This is mainly due to the burning of fossil fuels. The fossil fuels, coal and natural gas, are used in power stations to generate electricity. In modern life, we use many electrical appliances every day for work and leisure, e.g. computers and games consoles. Most motor vehicles are powered by a combustion engine that is fuelled by petrol or diesel, which are produced from fossil fuels. Deforestation is another man-made problem that is leading to increased levels of carbon dioxide. Forests play an important role in the natural removal of carbon dioxide during photosynthesis. As forests are cut down, this natural carbon dioxide sink is being removed.

2. (a) 1908

   (b) The numbers generally decrease from about 24 per 100 000 population in 1908 to zero in 1945 **[1]**. The most rapid decline in deaths was seen in the first 10 years after chlorine was introduced, when the number of deaths decreased by over half **[1]**.

   (c) The chlorine killed the microorganism present in the water that caused typhoid fever.

   (d) The data in the graph does show a correlation between chlorinated water and typhoid fever, but on its own there is insufficient data to make the absolute claim **[1]**. By looking at the graph alone, it is impossible to say if drugs / vaccinations **[or any other appropriate factor]** might have affected death rates for typhoid fever **[1]**. To be certain, more data is needed, for example similar data from a different country. If it showed the same result,

then this would strengthen the theory **[1]**. If experiments carried out directly on the microorganism responsible for typhoid fever showed positive results, this would add further evidence of a correlation **[1]**.

3. Hydrogen gas; Chlorine gas; **and** Sodium hydroxide **should be ticked.**

4. (a) The biodegradable bags are considerably weaker than the other two.

   (b) Find the range of the values, disregarding any outliers **[1]**, and calculate the mean (average) **[1]**.

   (c) 26.70N

   (d) $(26.50 + 26.53 + 26.49) \div 3 = 26.51N$ **[1 mark for correct working but wrong answer.]**

   (e) $(23.48 + 23.45 + 23.49 + 23.46) \div 4 = 23.47N$ **[1 mark for correct working but wrong answer.]**

   (f) **This is a model answer which would score full marks:** The manager should choose the polythene bag because it is stronger than the UV-degradable bag and will allow people to carry heavier shopping. Biodegradable bags are even weaker than UV-degradable bags, so would be less useful for carrying heavy shopping. Some members of the public think UV-degradable bags are the strongest, so the manager will have to explain that this is not what the data suggests. Polythene is not biodegradable, but it can be re-used and eventually recycled. Therefore, it may never end up in landfill. **[The UV-degradable bag could also be given as an acceptable answer, so long as it is well written and supported by valid arguments.]**

Answers

Modules P1–P3 (Pages 85–86)

1. (a) | C | A | B | D | F | E |

   [1 mark for each correctly placed letter up to a maximum of 5.]

  (b) Five thousand million years

  (c) 300 000km/s

  (d) The distance that light travels in one year.

2. (a) **Radio waves** – Microwaves – **Infrared** – Visible spectrum – **Ultraviolet** – X-rays – **Gamma rays**

  (b) **Any three from:** Sunburn; Skin ageing; Cancer; Kill / Damage cells

  (c) Ultraviolet **[1]**, X-rays **[1]**, gamma rays **[1]** are ionising. Ionising means that the radiation has high enough photon energy to remove an electron from an atom or molecule **[1]**.

3. (a) A resource that will not run out as it can be quickly and easily replaced

  (b) A resource that cannot be replaced within a lifetime

  (c) Wind, Wood **and** Tidal water **should be ticked.**

  (d) **This is a model answer which would score full marks:** Burning all fossil fuels releases carbon dioxide, a greenhouse gas, into the atmosphere. The heat released from burning fossil fuels is used to boil water, and water vapour, another greenhouse gas, is released into the atmosphere. Greenhouse gases trap heat from the Sun, causing average global temperatures to rise. This is called global warming. Global warming is likely to cause polar ice caps to melt, raising sea levels and flooding low-lying areas, as well as causing more extreme weather events like hurricanes.

  (e) 2000 × 60 = 120 000J
[1 mark for correct working but wrong answer.]

4. The movement of the observed wavelength of light towards the red end of the spectrum **[1]**. It tells us that the Universe is expanding **[1]**.

5. (a) Convection currents in the mantle **[1]** cause tectonic plate movement above **[1]**. The tectonic plates try to move towards / past / away from each other, causing a build-up of pressure **[1]**. The sudden release of pressure causes a jolting movement that triggers an earthquake **[1]**.

  (b) **This is a model answer which would score full marks:** The Mid-Atlantic Ridge is a constructive plate boundary. This means that the tectonic plates are moving away from each other. Molten rock rises to the surface, where it solidifies to form new ocean floor. As the rock solidifies, the direction of the Earth's magnetic field is recorded by the rock, as it is magnetised in one direction. The Earth's magnetic field reverses periodically, so there is a striped pattern of rocks either side of the Mid-Atlantic Ridge which is symmetrical. The width of each stripe indicates how long the Earth's magnetic field was orientated in a particular direction.

  (c) A few centimetres

Glossary

Acid – an aqueous compound with a pH value less than 7.

Adaptation – the gradual change of a particular organism over generations to become better suited to its environment.

Alkali – a substance that has a pH value higher than 7.

Allele – an alternative version of a gene.

Amplitude – the maximum disturbance caused by a wave from the equilibrium position.

Analogue – a signal that varies continuously in amplitude / frequency; can take any value.

Antibody – a protein produced by white blood cells to inactivate disease-causing microorganisms.

Antigen – a marker on a cell surface or on the surface of a disease-causing microorganism.

Antimicrobial – a chemical that kills (or inhibits the growth of) bacteria, fungi and viruses. Antibiotics and antivirals are examples.

Artery – a blood vessel that carries blood away from the heart.

Asexual reproduction – cells divide into two identical daughter cells that are also identical to the parent cell.

Atmosphere – the layer of gases surrounding the Earth.

Atom – the smallest part of an element that can enter into a chemical reaction.

Autotroph – an organism that makes its own food.

Biodegradable – a word that describes a material that can be broken down by bacteria.

Biodiversity – the variety of living organisms in an ecosystem.

Biomass – the mass of living matter in a living organism.

Blood pressure – the force of blood exerted on the inside walls of blood vessels.

Bone – rigid connective tissue that makes up the human skeleton.

Capillary – a blood vessel that connects arteries to veins; where the exchange of materials takes place.

Carrier wave – a wave that carries a signal.

Catalyst – a substance that is used to speed up a chemical reaction without being chemically altered itself.

Cell – the fundamental unit of a living organism.

Central nervous system (CNS) – the brain and spinal cord; allows an organism to react to its surroundings and coordinates its responses.

Chemical synthesis – the process by which many useful products are made.

Chromosome – a coil of DNA made up of genes, found in the nucleus of plant / animal cells.

Clone – a genetically identical offspring of an organism.

Combustion – a chemical reaction that occurs when fuels burn, releasing heat.

Compound – a substance in which the atoms of two or more elements are chemically joined, either by ionic or covalent bonds.

Contamination – contact with or internalisation of radioactive materials, for example by ingesting, inhaling, injecting or being covered in radioactive materials.

Covalent bond – the force of attraction between two atoms sharing electrons.

Cross-links – strong links between polymer chains.

Decomposition – the process of rotting or breaking down.

Digital – a signal that uses binary code to represent information; has two states: on (1) and off (0).

Displacement – the straight line distance between two points. It can be positive or negative.

Distillation – the process of separating a liquid from a mixture by boiling the mixture to evaporate the liquid and then condensing the vapours.

DNA (deoxyribonucleic acid) – the nucleic acid molecules that make up chromosomes and carry genetic information; found in every cell of every organism; control cell chemistry.

Ecosystem – the living biological and non-living physical components of the environment.

Effector – the part of the body, e.g. a muscle or a gland, which produces a response to a stimulus.

Electrolysis – the process by which an electric current causes a solution, containing ions, to undergo chemical decomposition.

Electron – a negatively charged particle that orbits the nucleus.

Element – a substance that consists of one type of atom.

Embryo – a ball of cells that will develop into a human / animal baby.

Enzyme – a protein molecule and biological catalyst found in living organisms that helps chemical reactions to take place (usually by increasing the rate of reaction).

Evaporation – the process in which a liquid changes into a gas by heating.

Evolve – to change naturally over a period of time.

Extinct – a species that has died out.

False negative – when a genetic test incorrectly states that the situation is normal (suggesting that the disease-causing allele is absent) when it is in fact positive.

False positive – when a genetic test incorrectly states that the result is positive (and therefore the disease-causing alleles are present) when in fact it is negative.

Fertilisation – the fusion of a male gamete with a female gamete.

Fetus – an unborn animal / human baby.

Filtration – a method for separating solids from liquids by passing a mixture through a porous material.

Food chain – a representation of the feeding relationship between organisms; energy is transferred up the chain.

Food web – the graphical representation of all the linked food chains in an ecosystem, allowing the identification of feeding relationships.

Force – a push or pull acting upon an object.

Frequency – the number of times that something happens in a set period of time; the number of times a wave oscillates in one second; measured in hertz.

Fossil fuel – fuel formed in the ground, over millions of years, from the remains of dead plants and animals.

Fuel – a substance that releases energy when burned in the presence of oxygen.

Gene – a small section of DNA, in a chromosome, that determines a particular characteristic; controls cellular activity by providing instructions (coding) for the production of a specific protein.

Genetic screening – the process of testing to see if certain genes are present.

Genetic test – a test to determine if an individual has a genetic disorder.

Genomics – the study of the genomes of organisms.

Global warming – the increase in the average temperature on Earth due to a rise in the level of greenhouse gases in the atmosphere.

Greenhouse effect – the increase in global temperature due to increased levels of greenhouse gases.

Greenhouse gas – a gas in the Earth's atmosphere that absorbs radiation and stops it from leaving the Earth's atmosphere.

Heart – a muscular organ that pumps blood around the body.

Heterotroph – an organism that is unable to make its own food; consumes other organisms.

Homeostasis – the maintenance of constant internal conditions in the body.

Hormone – a chemical messenger, made in ductless glands, which travels around the body in the blood to affect target organs elsewhere in the body.

Hydrocarbon – a compound made of carbon and hydrogen atoms only.

Immunity – the individual is protected against infection from a specific microorganism by their immune system.

Glossary

Intensive farming – a method of farming that uses artificial pesticides and fertilisers and controlled environments to maximize food production.

Irradiation – exposure to ionising radiation.

IVF (*in vitro* fertilisation) – a technique in which egg cells are fertilised outside the woman's body.

Kinetic energy – the energy possessed by an object because of its movement.

Life cycle assessment (LCA) – an analysis of a product from manufacture to disposal.

Lithosphere – the rigid outer layer of the Earth made up of the crust and the part of the mantle just below it.

Longitudinal wave – an energy-carrying wave in which the movement of the particles is in line with the direction in which the energy is being transferred.

Monomers – small molecules that join together to form polymers.

Muscle – tissue that can contract and relax to produce movement.

Nanoparticle – a particle that is less than 100nm in size.

Nanoscale – things relating to or occurring on a scale of nanometres.

Nanoscience – the science of structures that are 1–100 nanometres in size.

Nanotechnology – a branch of technology dealing with the manufacture of objects with dimensions of less than 100nm and the manipulation of individual molecules and atoms.

Natural selection – the process by which organisms that are better adapted to their environment are able to survive and reproduce, passing on their characteristics to their offspring.

Nitrification – the conversion of ammonia to nitrite and then to nitrate by microorganisms.

Nuclear fission – the splitting of atomic nuclei, which is accompanied by a release in energy.

Nuclear fusion – light nuclei join to form a heavier nucleus, releasing energy.

Nuclear reactor – the place where fission occurs in a nuclear power station.

Nucleus – the membrane-bound organelle where DNA is stored – it is the control centre of a cell; the core of an atom.

Outlier – a measured result that appears to be very different from the value you would expect or from other measured results. Therefore you strongly suggest that it is wrong.

Oxidation – a chemical reaction that occurs when oxygen joins with an element or compound.

Parallax – the apparent motion of an object against a background.

pH – a measure of acidity or alkalinity.

Photon – a 'packet' of energy carried by electromagnetic radiation.

Photosynthesis – the chemical process that takes place in green plants where water combines with carbon dioxide to produce glucose using light energy.

Phylogenetic tree – a graphical representation of the evolutionary relationships between living things based on analysis of DNA.

Placebo – an inert (non-effective) dummy pill or treatment.

Pollutant – a chemical that can harm the environment and health.

Polymer – a long-chain hydrocarbon molecule built up from small units called monomers.

Potential difference (voltage) – the difference in electrical energy carried by the charge between two points.

Receptor – the part of the nervous system that detects a stimulus; a sense organ, e.g. eyes, ears, nose, etc.

Recycling – to reuse materials that would otherwise be considered waste.

Redshift – the shift of light towards the red part of the visible spectrum; shows that the Universe is expanding.

Reduction – a chemical reaction that occurs when oxygen is removed.

Refraction – the change in direction and speed of a wave as it passes from one material to another.

Glossary

Renewable resources – resources that can be replaced as quickly as they are used up.

Respiration – the liberation of energy from food.

Ribosome – a small structure found in the cytoplasm of living cells, where protein synthesis takes place.

Salt – the product of a chemical reaction between a base and an acid.

Selective breeding – the process by which animals are selected and mated to produce offspring with desirable characteristics (artificial selection).

Sexual reproduction – reproduction involving the fusing together of gametes formed via meiosis.

Signal – any communication that carries a message.

Solar system – a collection of stars and planets.

Soluble – a property that means a substance can dissolve in a solvent.

Solution – the mixture formed when a solute dissolves in a solvent.

Specialised – developed or adapted for a specific function.

Species – a group of organisms capable of breeding to produce fertile offspring.

Speed – how far an object travels in a given time.

Stem cell – a cell that can give rise to specialised cells.

Sustainable – capable of being continued with minimal long-term effect on the environment; resources that can be replaced or maintained.

Symptom – a visible or noticeable effect of a disease, illness or injury.

Tectonic plates – huge sections of the Earth's crust that move relative to one another.

Transformer – an electrical device used to change the voltage of alternating currents.

Transverse wave – a wave in which the oscillations (vibrations) are at 90° to the direction of energy transfer.

Universe – billions of galaxies.

Vaccine – a liquid preparation used to make the body produce antibodies to provide protection against disease.

Variation – the differences between individuals of the same species.

Vein – a type of blood vessel that transports blood towards the heart.

Voltage (potential difference) – the difference in electrical energy carried by the charge between two points.

Wavelength – the distance between corresponding points on two adjacent disturbances (waves).

Zygote – the first cell formed after the fertilisation of an egg by a sperm.

Periodic Table

1	2												3	4	5	6	7	0
																		4 **He** helium 2
39 **K** potassium 19	40 **Ca** calcium 20	45 **Sc** scandium 21	48 **Ti** titanium 22	51 **V** vanadium 23	52 **Cr** chromium 24	55 **Mn** manganese 25	56 **Fe** iron 26	59 **Co** cobalt 27	59 **Ni** nickel 28	63.5 **Cu** copper 29	65 **Zn** zinc 30	12 **C** carbon 6	14 **N** nitrogen 7	16 **O** oxygen 8	19 **F** fluorine 9	20 **Ne** neon 10

| 85
Rb
rubidium
37 | 88
Sr
strontium
38 | 89
Y
yttrium
39 | 91
Zr
zirconium
40 | 93
Nb
niobium
41 | 96
Mo
molybdenum
42 | [98]
Tc
technetium
43 | 101
Ru
ruthenium
44 | 103
Rh
rhodium
45 | 106
Pd
palladium
46 | 108
Ag
silver
47 | 112
Cd
cadmium
48 | 28
Si
silicon
14 | 31
P
phosphorus
15 | 32
S
sulfur
16 | 35.5
Cl
chlorine
17 | 40
Ar
argon
18 |

| 133
Cs
caesium
55 | 137
Ba
barium
56 | 139
La*
lanthanum
57 | 178
Hf
hafnium
72 | 181
Ta
tantalum
73 | 184
W
tungsten
74 | 186
Re
rhenium
75 | 190
Os
osmium
76 | 192
Ir
iridium
77 | 195
Pt
platinum
78 | 197
Au
gold
79 | 201
Hg
mercury
80 | 31
Ga
gallium
31 | 73
Ge
germanium
32 | 75
As
arsenic
33 | 79
Se
selenium
34 | 80
Br
bromine
35 |

| 70
Ga
gallium
31 | 115
In
indium
49 | 119
Sn
tin
50 | 122
Sb
antimony
51 | 128
Te
tellurium
52 | 127
I
iodine
53 | 131
Xe
xenon
54 |

| [223]
Fr
francium
87 | [226]
Ra
radium
88 | [227]
Ac*
actinium
89 | [261]
Rf
rutherfordium
104 | [262]
Db
dubnium
105 | [266]
Sg
seaborgium
106 | [264]
Bh
bohrium
107 | [277]
Hs
hassium
108 | [268]
Mt
meitnerium
109 | [271]
Ds
darmstadtium
110 | [272]
Rg
roentgenium
111 | 204
Tl
thallium
81 | 207
Pb
lead
82 | 209
Bi
bismuth
83 | [209]
Po
polonium
84 | [210]
At
astatine
85 | [222]
Rn
radon
86 |

Elements with atomic numbers 112–116 have been reported but not fully authenticated

The lanthanoids (atomic numbers 58–71) and the actinoids (atomic numbers 90–103) have been omitted.

The relative atomic masses of copper and chlorine have not been rounded to the nearest whole number.

Notes

Notes

Index

Index